I0152114

Collected Works of René Guénon

Studies in Dante and Christian Esoterism

RENÉ GUÉNON

Studies in Dante
and
Christian Esoterism

SOPHIA PERENNIS

First published in French (2 volumes):
L'Ésotérisme de Dante
© Éditions Gallimard 1925, 1957
Aperçus sur l'Ésotérisme chrétien
© Les Éditions Traditionnelles 1954
English translations © Sophia Perennis 2001
First English edition in (2 volumes) 2001
The Esoterism of Dante
Insights into Christian Esoterism
© Sophia Perennis 2001
Second Impression 2004
Combined edition with new Foreword:
Studies in Dante and Christian Esoterism
© Sophia Perennis 2025

All rights reserved

Series editor: James R. Wetmore

No part of this book may be reproduced or transmitted,
in any form or by any means, without permission

For information, address:
Sophia Perennis, PO Box 931
Philmont NY 12565

ISBN 978 1 59731 246 2 (pbk)
ISBN 978 1 59731 247 9 (cloth)

The publisher gives special thanks to
Henry D., Jennie L., & Samuel D. Fohr
for making this edition possible

Contents

Editorial Note

René Guénon (1886–1951) is undoubtedly one of the luminaries of the twentieth century, whose critique of the modern world has stood fast against the shifting sands of recent philosophies. His *oeuvre* of twenty-six volumes is providential for the modern seeker: pointing ceaselessly to the Perennial Wisdom found in past cultures ranging from the Shamanistic to the Indian and Chinese, the Hellenic and Judaic, the Christian and Islamic, and including also Alchemy, Hermeticism, and other esoteric currents, at the same time it directs the reader to the deepest level of religious *praxis*, emphasizing the need for affiliation with a revealed tradition even while acknowledging the final identity of all spiritual paths as they approach the summit of spiritual realization. One of René Guénon's lifelong quests was to discover, or revive, the esoteric, initiatory dimension of the Christian tradition.

Especially since the Renaissance, some in Western Christendom have suspected that the deeper dimension of their tradition has somehow been lost, and have therefore sought to discover, or create, an 'esoteric' or 'initiatic' Christianity. In the middle of the nineteenth century two scholars, Gabriele Rossetti and Eugène Aroux, pointed to certain esoteric meanings in the work of Dante Alighieri, notably *The Divine Comedy*. Partly based on their scholarship, Guénon in 1925 published *The Esoterism of Dante*, included as Part III in the present volume, in which he details Dante's knowledge of traditional sciences unknown to the moderns: the sciences of numbers, cosmic cycles, and sacred astrology. From the theses of Rossetti and Aroux, Guénon retains only those elements that prove the existence of such esoteric teachings; but he also makes clear that esoterism is not 'heresy' and that a doctrine reserved for an elite can be superimposed on the teaching given the faithful without standing in opposition to it. A collection of related articles was published posthumously in 1954 under the title *Insights into Christian Esoterism* (to

i

which a separate monograph, *Saint Bernard*, is added). In these articles, comprising Parts I and II of the present edition, Guénon undertakes to establish that the three parts of *The Divine Comedy* represent the stages of initiatic realization, exploring the parallels between the symbolism of the *Commedia* and that of Freemasonry, Rosicrucianism, and Christian Hermeticism. Here Guénon also touches on the all-important question of Medieval esoterism and discusses the role of sacred languages and the principle of initiation in the Christian tradition, as well as such esoteric Christian themes and organizations as the Holy Grail, the Guardians of the Holy Land, the Sacred Heart, the Fedeli d'Amore and the 'Courts of Love', and the Secret Language of Dante.

***

Guénon often uses words or expressions set off in 'scare quotes'. To avoid clutter, single quotation marks have been used throughout. As for transliterations, Guénon was more concerned with phonetic fidelity than academic usage. The system adopted here reflects the views of scholars familiar both with the languages and Guénon's writings. Brackets indicate editorial insertions, or, within citations, Guénon's additions. Wherever possible, references have been updated, and English editions substituted.

This translation was made specifically for the Collected Works of René Guénon edition. The publisher would like to acknowledge the assistance in this project of Henry Fohr, Cecil Bethell, Jacques Phillipe, Marie Hansen, Patrick Moore, John Champoux, John Herlihy, Hubert and Rohini Schiff, Brian Keeble, William Stoddart, Rob Baker, and William Quinn.

Foreword

René Guénon (1886–1951) left a considerable literary legacy: seventeen books published during his lifetime and hundreds of articles and reviews published in various periodicals, principally the Catholic review *Regnabit* and *Études Traditionnelles* (formerly *Le Voile d'Isis*), for which he provided the inspiration from 1929 onward. The majority of these articles and reviews have since been collected in six posthumous volumes. The present collection includes certain studies that appeared at various times, but share a common reference to the subject of Christian esoterism. This is not to say that these studies systematically treat, even in summary fashion, the different aspects of this important subject, which Guénon never set out to present in a didactic manner. They are, rather, occasional pieces whose point of departure was furnished either by readers' questions or by works with which Guénon was familiar, works whose errors or insufficiencies he felt obliged to point out. Fragmentary though they are, the interest of these articles seems all the greater, since Guénon devoted no single work to Christianity—the traditional form that rightly preoccupied the great majority of his readers. Guénon's reserve in this respect is closely related to the role he assigns in *East and West* and *The Crisis of the Modern World* to the Western 'elect'. This role consists principally in a synthetic exposé of the Eastern metaphysical doctrines, destined to awaken in intellectually qualified Westerners the desire to rediscover and in some measure bring to light the profounder aspects of their own tradition—it being incumbent on such Westerners, in Guénon's view, to show that the intellectual and spiritual degeneracy of the West is not so total and irremediable that no hope of redress remains. It was only natural, therefore, that he restricted himself to providing certain keys and pointers for further research as far as the Christian tradition is concerned.

Guénon's attitude in this respect (quite understandable in itself) was met by a wide diversity of interpretations from readers with superficial and incomplete knowledge of the Guénonian *oeuvre*, as also from critics who were perhaps not always disinterested. It seemed necessary therefore to collect together in this present volume those texts in which Guénon most clearly stated his position with regard to Christianity.[1] Another important text from this point of view (not included in the present volume) is *The King of the World*, in which Guénon, assimilating the three Magi of the Gospels to the three chiefs of the Supreme Spiritual Center, writes:

> The homage rendered in this way to the newborn Christ by the authentic representatives of the Primordial Tradition in the three worlds which are their respective domains, is at the same time, we should clearly note, the assurance of the perfect orthodoxy of Christianity in this respect.

Speaking elsewhere of this event in sacred history, Guénon expresses the same idea with more precision. Having alluded to Melchizedek, who appears in the Bible invested with both priestly and royal qualities, he writes:

> Finally, Melchizedek is not the only personage in Holy Scripture who appears with the double nature of priest and king. In the New Testament, in fact, we find the union of these two functions again in the Magi. This might lead us to think that there is a quite direct line between them and Melchizedek, or in other words that in both cases we have to do with representatives of the same single authority. Now, by the homage they accord to Christ and by the gifts they offer him, the Magi expressly recognize in him the source of that authority in all the domains where it is exercised: the first offers him gold and salutes him as king; the second offers him incense and salutes him as priest; the third,

---

1. These texts were first published in French as three separate volumes: *Aperçus sur l'Ésotérisme chrétien*, *L'Ésotérisme de Dante*, and the brochure *Saint Bernard*. They were first published in English by Sophia Perennis as two texts: *Insights into Christian Esoterism* (in which the brochure on Saint Bernard was included), and *The Esoterism of Dante*.

finally, offers him myrrh, the balm of incorruptibility, and salutes him as prophet or spiritual Master par excellence, which corresponds directly to the common principle of the two powers, sacerdotal and royal. From the moment of his human birth, homage is thus rendered to Christ in the 'three worlds' of which all the Eastern doctrines speak: the terrestrial world, the intermediary world, and the celestial world; and those who render that homage are none other than the authentic depositories of the Primordial Tradition, the guardians entrusted with the revelation made to humanity in the Terrestrial Paradise. Such at least is the conclusion that, for us, clearly emerges from a comparison of the corresponding testimonies to be found on this point among all peoples. Moreover, under the varying forms it assumes during the course of time, under the more or less opaque veils that sometimes conceal it from the gaze of those who hold to external appearances, this great Primordial Tradition has in reality always been the sole true religion of all humanity. Should we not therefore regard the step taken by the representatives of that tradition, as related in the Gospel (if we would understand it truly), as one of the most beautiful proofs of the divinity of Christ, and at the same time as a decisive recognition of the supreme priesthood and royalty that truly appertains to him 'according to the Order of Melchizedek'?

Indeed, the Christianity René Guénon was thinking of is not that of the pseudo-esoterists, who see in Christ no more than a 'great initiate'; and no more is it that of the liberal Protestants. It is, rather, the authentic Christianity of the Apostolic Churches. As he writes in *The Crisis of the Modern World*:

Protestantism is illogical: while doing all it can to 'humanize' religion, it nevertheless, in theory at least, retains revelation, which is a supra-human element. It does not dare carry its negation to the logical conclusion but, by subjecting revelation to all the discussions resulting from purely human interpretations, it does in fact reduce it to next to nothing; and seeing, as one does, people who persist in calling themselves Christian even though they deny the very divinity of Christ, one cannot avoid the supposition that they are much nearer to complete negation than to real Christianity.

A few lines further on, Guénon's position becomes still clearer:

An objection might here be raised: although it broke away from the Catholic organization, might not Protestantism, in that it continued to admit the validity of the Sacred Books, have preserved the traditional doctrine contained therein? But the introduction of 'free criticism' completely refutes such a hypothesis, since it opens the door to all manner of individual fantasies; moreover, the preservation of the doctrine presupposes an organized traditional teaching to keep alive the orthodox interpretation, and in actual fact this teaching has, in the Western world, been identified with Catholicism.

And as Guénon then points out, what was true at the time of the Reformation is still true today:

It is moreover quite certain . . . that it is in Catholicism alone that all that may still remain of the traditional spirit in the West has been preserved; but does this mean that—in Catholicism at least—one can speak of an integral conservation of tradition completely untainted by the modern spirit? Unfortunately this does not appear to be the case; or, more precisely, if the deposit of tradition has remained intact—which is in itself much—it is doubtful whether its deeper meaning is fully understood, even by a restricted elect, which, if it existed, would doubtless show itself either in action or in influence, neither of which in fact is anywhere to be seen. Most probably therefore there is only what might be termed a preservation of the tradition in a latent state, in which state it is always possible for those who are capable of it to rediscover its meaning, even though no one may be fully aware of it at the present time.

The preceding quotations, however important they may be, nevertheless call for further clarification. Given that Christianity occupies relatively little place in Guénon's work as a whole, and that he did not apply himself to the task of bringing to light its metaphysical and initiatic content, certain people have believed themselves entitled to conclude that Guénon considered Christianity, although undeniably a regular and orthodox form, as in some way incomplete with regard to metaphysical knowledge. Guénon declared himself opposed to such a misconstruction of his thought right from the outset. In 1925, in his lengthy article *Eastern Metaphysics*, Guénon made a declaration that leaves no room for ambiguity on this point. After speaking of the 'partial metaphysics' of Aristotle and his successors, he writes:

> For or our part, we are certain that there was something other than this in the West, both in Antiquity and in the Middle Ages; that there were, for the use of an elect, purely metaphysical doctrines that we may call complete—comprising that realization which, for most of our contemporaries, is no doubt almost inconceivable.

Now, in the West and in the Middle Ages (and we know that when Guénon speaks of the Middle Ages he has in mind above all the period of the Latin Middle Ages, extending from the reign of Charlemagne to the beginning of the fourteenth century), these complete and purely metaphysical doctrines, as well as the corresponding methods of realization, could only depend on Christian esoterism and, more precisely, on an esoterism based on the religious exoterism of Roman Catholicism, of which perhaps the most important testimony that has come down to us from the Middle Ages is the work of Meister Eckhart; and these doctrines assuredly had their equivalent in Eastern Christianity. It is thanks to Guénon's writings that many of our contemporaries have been able to rediscover and correctly interpret these generally forgotten or ill-understood doctrines.

The studies brought together in the present volume are, for the most part, devoted to organizations that Guénon considered to have been responsible, in the Middle Ages, for extending the teaching and methods of Christian esoterism: the Order of the Temple, the Fideli d'Amore, and the Knighthood of the Holy Grail. They are preceded with two studies, entitled 'Concerning Sacred Languages' and 'Christianity and Initiation'. The first, which brings to light the importance of the Hebrew language in Christianity, indicates perhaps the most important way forward for profound research in the traditional sciences and the methods of Christian esoterism. The second concerns the very structure of Christianity, both in its religious and its initiatic aspects.

In conclusion, it seems to us indispensable here to formulate a question that will spring to mind for many readers once they have acquainted themselves with this present work: has esoterism, in its purity if not its integrality, remained living somewhere at the heart of Latin Christianity? In a note written late in life, Guénon envisages this possibility. And why should this astonish us? Let us refer to some words we ought not to forget. On the one hand:

> And I say also unto thee that thou art Peter, and upon this rock I will build my Church, and the gates of Hell shall not prevail against it.

And on the other:

> Turning round, Peter saw, following them, the disciple whom Jesus loved, the one who at the Supper had leaned upon His breast.... Peter therefore, seeing him, said to Jesus, 'Lord, and what of this man?' Jesus said to him, 'If I wish him to remain until I come, what is it to thee? Do thou follow me.' This saying therefore went abroad among the brethren, that that disciple was not to die. But Jesus had not said to him, 'He is not to die', but rather, 'If I wish him to remain until I come, what is that to thee?'

The work of René Guénon certainly does not contradict this.

JEAN REYOR

PART I

Structure and Characteristics of the Christian Tradition

1

Concerning
Sacred Languages

We have had previous occasion[1] to point out that the Western world
has at its disposal no other sacred language than Hebrew, which is
certainly quite a strange fact, and one that invites certain observations; for even if we cannot claim to resolve the diverse questions
that arise on this subject, it is not devoid of interest. It is evident
that if Hebrew can play this role in the West, it is because of the
direct filiation that exists between the Judaic and Christian traditions and the incorporation of the Hebrew Scriptures into the
sacred books of Christianity itself; but one may wonder how it happens that Christianity possesses no sacred language of its own, a
truly exceptional fact that sets it apart from other traditions.

Here it is especially important not to confuse sacred languages
with those that are simply liturgical:[2] for a language to fulfill this
latter role, it is enough that it be 'fixed', exempt from the continual
variations that vernacular languages necessarily undergo,[3] whereas
sacred languages are exclusively those in which the scriptures of the

---

1. 'The Roots of Plants', *Symbols of Sacred Science* (first published in English as
Fundamental Symbols: The Universal Language of Sacred Science), chap. 62.
2. This is all the more important in that we have seen an orientalist qualify Arabic as a 'liturgical language', whereas it is really a sacred language, apparently with
the hidden intention (clear enough to anyone with understanding) of disparaging
the Islamic tradition; and this is not unrelated to the fact that this same orientalist
has conducted a veritable campaign for the adoption of Latin script in Arabic-
speaking countries.
3. We prefer to say 'fixed' language rather than the more customary 'dead' language because, from the traditional point of view, as long as a language is used in
rituals, one cannot say that it is really dead.

different traditions are expressed. It is evident from this that every sacred language is at the same time, and with all the more reason, the liturgical or ritual language of the tradition to which it belongs,[4] but the inverse is not true. Thus, Greek and Latin, along with certain other ancient languages,[5] may perfectly well play the role of liturgical language for Christianity,[6] but they are in no way sacred languages in themselves; even were we to suppose that they may once have had such a character,[7] it would have been in traditions that are now lost and with which Christianity obviously has no affiliation.

The absence of a sacred language in Christianity becomes even more striking when we observe that the original text of the Hebrew Scriptures, which still exists, serves 'officially' only as a basis for the Greek and Latin translations.[8] As for the New Testament, only the Greek text is known, and it is from this that all versions in other languages, even the Hebrew and the Syriac, were made; now it is surely impossible to maintain, at least with regard to the Gospels, that this is their true language — that is to say, the language in which Christ's own words were spoken. Nevertheless it is possible that they were only written in Greek after having been previously transmitted orally in the original language;[9] but one may then ask why, when they came to be fixed in writing, this could not just as well have been

4. We say 'liturgical or ritual' because the first of these two words strictly applies only to religious forms, whereas the second has an altogether general significance that is applicable equally to all traditions.

5. Notably Syrian, Coptic, and Old Slavonic, currently in use in various Eastern Churches.

6. It should be clear that we have in mind only the regular and orthodox branches of Christianity; Protestantism in all its forms makes use only of vernacular languages and so has no liturgy strictly speaking.

7. The fact that we know of no sacred books written in these languages does not entitle us to reject this supposition absolutely, for much from antiquity has certainly not survived. There are questions that would certainly be very difficult to resolve at present, for instance regarding the Roman tradition, the true character of the Sybilline Books, and the language in which they were written.

8. The Septuagint and the Vulgate.

9. This simple remark on the subject of oral transmission should suffice to nullify all the discussions of the 'critics' on the alleged dating of the Gospels, and this would be a sufficient refutation if the defenders of Christianity were not themselves more or less affected by the anti-traditional spirit of the modern world.

done in the original language, a question in fact difficult to answer. Whatever the reasons for this it all presents several difficulties, for only a sacred language can ensure the rigorous invariability of the scriptural texts since translations necessarily vary from one language to another, and are in any case never more than approximate since each language has its own modes of expression, which do not correspond exactly with those of any other.[10] Even when the exterior and literal sense is rendered as clearly as possible, there are still many obstacles to penetrating into the other, deeper meanings.[11] From this we can appreciate some of the special difficulties that the study of the Christian tradition presents to anyone who does not wish to restrict himself simply to more or less superficial appearances.

Of course this is not at all to say that there are no reasons why Christianity has this exceptional characteristic of being a tradition without a sacred language; on the contrary, there certainly must be reasons; but we need to recognize that they are not at first apparent, and it would doubtless entail a very considerable labor — which we cannot think of undertaking here — to bring them to light. Moreover, almost everything touching upon the origins and earliest years of Christianity is unfortunately shrouded in obscurity. We might also ask if there is not a connection between this characteristic and another that is hardly less singular: that Christianity possesses no equivalent to the properly 'legal' aspect of other traditions, so much so that to supply one it was forced to adapt ancient Roman law for its own use, making additions which, though proper to it, are nonetheless not based on the Gospels.[12] If on the one hand we bring

10. This state of affairs is not unfavorable to the attacks of the modernist 'exegetes'; even if texts in a sacred language existed, that would doubtless not prevent such 'exegetes' from discussing them in their profane way, but at least it would then be easier for all those who still retain something of the traditional spirit not to feel obliged to take their claims into account.

11. This is particularly evident in sacred languages, where the characters have a numerical or properly hieroglyphic value that often has a great importance from this point of view, and of which an ordinary translation can obviously convey nothing.

12. One could use a term borrowed from the Islamic tradition and say that Christianity has no *sharī'ah*. This is all the more remarkable because in what could be called the 'Abrahamic' filiation it is situated between Judaism and Islam, both of which on the contrary have a highly elaborated *sharī'ah*.

these two facts together, and if on the other we bear in mind that, as we have frequently pointed out, certain Christian rites seem in some degree to be 'exteriorizations' of initiatic rites, we could even ask whether the original Christianity was not in reality something very different from what it seems to be at present — if not in respect of the doctrine itself,[13] at least as to the ends in view of which it was established.[14] For our part, our only wish has been to pose these questions, to which we certainly do not attempt to offer an answer; but given their obvious interest in more than one connection, it is much to be hoped that those with the time and means for the necessary research may one day throw some light on the subject.

13. Or perhaps we should rather say, of that part of the doctrine that has remained generally known up to our time; this has certainly not changed, but it is also possible that there may have been other teachings, for certain allusions made by the Church Fathers seem scarcely comprehensible otherwise. The efforts made by the moderns to minimize the significance of these allusions ultimately only prove the limitations of their own mentality.

14. The study of these questions would also raise the question of links between primitive Christianity and the Essenes, about whom, moreover, very little is known, but it is at least established that they formed an esoteric organization attached to Judaism; many fanciful things have been said on this subject, but it is still a point meriting serious examination.

2

Christianity and Initiation

We did not mean to return here to questions concerning the character of Christianity itself, for we thought that what we had said of this on other occasions, however incidentally, was more or less sufficient to preclude any ambiguity on the subject.[1] Unfortunately, we have lately had to note that this is not at all the case and that certain rather troublesome confusions have arisen in the minds of many of our readers, making clear the need to further elucidate certain points. It is furthermore only with regret that we do this, for we must confess that we have never felt any inclination to give this subject special treatment. There are several reasons for this, the first being the almost impenetrable obscurity that surrounds everything relating to the origins and early stages of Christianity, an obscurity so profound that, upon reflection, it seems impossible that it should simply have been accidental, but more likely was expressly intended — an observation to be kept in mind in connection with what we shall have to say later.

Despite all the difficulties resulting from such a state of affairs,

---

1. We could not help being somewhat surprised upon learning that some readers think that our *Perspectives on Initiation* deals more directly and extensively with Christianity than our other works do; we can assure them that there as elsewhere we meant to speak of it only to the extent necessary to make our exposition comprehensible, and, one might say, as a function of the various questions we had to treat. Scarcely less astonishing is the fact that some readers who assure us they have attentively followed all we have written should nevertheless think this book contains something new on that score, whereas on all the points they have brought to our attention in this respect we were on the contrary only reiterating considerations we had already developed in some of our earlier articles in *Le Voile d'Isis* and *Études Traditionnelles*.

there is nevertheless at least one point that does not seem to be in doubt, one that has in any event not been contested by any who have shared their observations with us, but that has, quite to the contrary, provided a support for certain of their objections. This point is that, far from being merely the religion or exoteric tradition known today, Christianity originally had both in its rites and doctrine an essentially esoteric and thus 'initiatic' character. We find confirmation of this in the fact that the Islamic tradition considers primitive Christianity to have been a *ṭarīqah*, that is, essentially an initiatic 'way', and not a *sharī'ah* or social legislation addressed to all; and this was so true that subsequently this latter had to be supplied by instituting a 'canon' law[2] that was really only an adaptation of ancient Roman law, thus something coming entirely from the outside, and not at all a development of something originally contained in Christianity itself. Moreover, it is evident that no prescription can be found in the Gospels that might be regarded as having a truly legal character in the proper sense of the word. The well-known say-ing, 'Render unto Caesar that which is Caesar's,' seems to us particu-larly significant in this respect because, regarding everything of an exterior order, it formally implies the acceptance of a legislation wholly foreign to Christianity. This legislation was simply that exist-ing in the milieu into which Christianity was born, given that it was at that time incorporated into the Roman Empire. This would surely have been a most serious lacuna if Christianity had been then what it later became, for the very existence of such a lacuna would have been not just inexplicable but truly inconceivable for a regular and orthodox tradition if Christianity had really included an exoter-ism as well as an esoterism, and if it was even to have applied—above all, one might say—to the exoteric domain. If, on the con-trary, Christianity had the character we have just attributed to it, the thing is easily explained because there is no question of a defect but rather an intention to abstain from

---

2. Apropos of this it is perhaps not without interest to note that in Arabic the word *qanūn*, derived from the Greek, is used to designate any law adopted for purely contingent reasons and not forming an integral part of the *sharī'ah*, or traditional legislation.

intervening in a domain that by definition could not concern it under these conditions.

For that to have been possible, the earliest Christian church would have had to be a closed or reserved organization to which admission would not have been granted indiscriminately, being reserved for those who possessed the qualifications necessary to receive initiation validly in what we might call a 'Christic' form; and we could doubtless find many more indications that such was indeed the case, although they would generally be misunderstood in our day, when the modern tendency to deny esoterism prompts many more or less consciously to deny these indications of their true significance.[3] In short, then, the Church would have been comparable to the Buddhist *Sangha*, admission to which also had the characteristics of a true initiation,[4] and which is commonly compared to a 'monastic order', an apt comparison at least in that its particular statutes, just as those of a monastic order in the Christian sense, were not made to extend to the whole of the society at the heart of which it was established.[5] From this point of view the case of Christianity is therefore not unique among the various known traditional forms, and it seems to us that this fact should diminish the astonishment that some may feel about it; it would perhaps be more difficult to explain how it could have undergone the complete change in character shown by everything we see around us; but this is not the moment to examine that question.

3. We have often had occasion to draw attention to this type of procedure in the current interpretations of the Church Fathers and more particularly of the Greek Fathers: every effort is made to maintain that it is a mistake to see esoteric allusions in their writings, and when that becomes altogether impossible there is no hesitation in holding it against them and declaring that there has been a regrettable lapse on their part!

4. See A.K. Coomaraswamy, 'L'ordination bouddhique est-elle une Initiation?', in the July 1939 issue of *Études Traditionnelles*.

5. It was this illegitimate extrapolation that later provoked certain deviations in Indian Buddhism, such as the negation of the castes; the Buddha did not have to take these into account within a closed organization whose members were bound, at least in principle, to be beyond caste distinction; but to wish to suppress that same distinction in the entire social milieu constituted a formal heresy from the Hindu point of view.

Here then is the objection that was addressed to us and to which we alluded above: since the Christian rites, and the sacraments in particular, had an initiatic character, how could they have lost this and become simply exoteric rites? This is impossible, even contradictory they tell us, because the initiatic character is permanent and immutable and could never be effaced, so that it need only be admitted that as a result of circumstances and of the admission of a great majority of unqualified individuals, what was originally an effective initiation was reduced to no more than a virtual one. Here there is a misapprehension that seems quite evident: initiation, as we have repeatedly explained, does indeed confer upon those who receive it a character that is acquired once and for all and is truly ineradicable; but this idea of the permanence of the initiatic character applies to the human beings who possess it and not to the action of the spiritual influence or to the rites that are intended to serve as its vehicle; it is absolutely unjustified to transfer this notion from one to the other, which amounts in the end to attributing to it an altogether different significance, and we are certain that we have never ourselves said anything that could provoke such a confusion. In support of their position, however, our opponents assert that the spiritual action is effected through the Christian sacraments by the Holy Spirit, which is perfectly true though totally beside the point; moreover, whether the spiritual influence is named according to Christian terminology or according to the terminology of some other tradition, it remains true that it is essentially transcendent and supra-individual, for were it not so we would no longer be dealing with a spiritual influence at all but merely a psychic one. Even admitting this, however, what could prevent the same influence, or one similar, from acting according to different modalities and in different domains as well? Furthermore, even if this influence belongs to the transcendent order, must its effects be such in every case?[6] We do not at all see why this should be so, and we are even certain of the contrary; indeed, we have always taken the greatest care to point

6. Let us note in passing that a particular consequence of this would be to preclude spiritual influences from producing effects relating simply to the corporeal order, such as miraculous cures, for example.

8

out that a spiritual influence intervenes as much in exoteric rites as in initiatic rites, but it goes without saying that the effects it produces could never be of the same order in the two cases, for otherwise the very distinction between the two corresponding domains would no longer exist.[7] Neither do we understand why it is inadmissible that the spiritual influence that works through the Christian sacraments, after having first acted in the initiatic order, should not in other conditions and for reasons contingent on these very conditions, then lower its action to the merely religious and exoteric domain, so that its effects were thenceforth limited to certain exclusively individual possibilities with the goal of 'salvation' while nevertheless preserving these same ritual supports as far as external appearances are concerned, because they were instituted by Christ and without them there would no longer have been any properly Christian tradition. That this may really have been the case, and that consequently in our present state of affairs (and indeed for quite a long time now) we can no longer in any way consider Christian rites to have an initiatic character, is something we will have to stress with greater precision; but we must also point out that there is a certain linguistic impropriety in saying that they 'lost' that character, as if that fact were purely accidental, for we think on the contrary that there must have been an adaptation that, despite the regrettable consequences it entailed in some respects, was fully justified, and even necessitated, by the circumstances of time and place.

If we consider the state of the Western world in the age in question (that is, of the territories comprised in the Roman Empire), it is easy to see that, had Christianity not 'descended' into the exoteric domain, this world would soon have been deprived of all tradition, for the traditions that had existed until that time, especially the Greco-Roman tradition, which naturally was predominant, had reached an advanced state of degeneration heralding the imminent

---

7. If the action of the Holy Spirit were exercised only in the esoteric domain, because this alone is truly transcendent, we would also ask our opponents, who are Catholics, what one should think of the doctrine stating that this influence operates in the formulation of the most clearly exoteric dogmas?

end of their cycle of existence.[8] This 'descent' therefore, let us insist again, was neither an accident nor a deviation but should on the contrary be regarded as having a truly 'providential' character since it prevented the West from falling at that time into a state comparable to that in which it now finds itself. The moment had not yet arrived for a general loss of tradition such as characterizes modern times; a 'rectification' was therefore necessary, and Christianity alone could accomplish it, but on the condition that it renounce the esoteric and 'restricted' character it originally possessed;[9] and thus the 'rectification' was not only beneficial for Western humanity—which is too obvious to require emphasis—but at the same time conformed perfectly with the cyclical laws themselves, as all 'providential' action intervening in the course of history necessarily does.

It would in all likelihood be impossible to assign a precise date to this change that made of Christianity a religion in the proper sense of the word, that is to say a traditional form addressing itself to all without distinction; but what is certain in any case is that it was already an established fact at the time of Constantine and the Council of Nicaea, so that the latter had only to 'sanction' it, so to speak, by inaugurating the era of 'dogmatic' formulations intended as a purely exoteric presentation of the doctrine.[10] This change could not but occasion certain drawbacks, for the enclosing of doctrine in

8. It should be understood that in speaking of the Western world in its entirety we make an exception for an elite that not only still understood its own tradition from the exterior point of view, but that continued to receive initiation into the mysteries; the tradition could thus have maintained itself for quite some time in an increasingly restricted setting; but this goes beyond the scope of our present topic since we are concerned with Westerners in general, for whom Christianity had to come to replace the old traditional forms at a time when they were being reduced to nothing more than 'superstitions' in the etymological sense of the word.

9. One might say in this regard that the transition from esoterism to exoterism constituted a veritable 'sacrifice', which is moreover true of every descent of the spirit.

10. At the same time the 'conversion' of Constantine implied, by a sort of official act of imperial authority, a recognition of the fact that the Greco-Roman tradition had thenceforth to be considered extinct, although naturally some remnants may have survived for a fairly long time—remnants that could only degenerate further and further until they finally disappeared and were later designated by the contemptuous term of 'paganism'.

clearly defined and limited formulas made it much more difficult, even for those who were capable of so doing, to penetrate its deeper meaning. Furthermore, truths of a more properly esoteric order, by their very nature beyond the reach of the vast majority, could then only be presented as 'mysteries' in the popular meaning this word has acquired, which is to say that before long they had to appear to the generality of men as things impossible to understand, indeed as things one was forbidden even to try and fathom. These drawbacks, however, were not such as could go against the establishment of Christianity in traditional exoteric form or put its legitimacy into question, given the immense advantage that would result for the Western world, as we have already said. Moreover, if Christianity as such ceased thenceforth to be initiatic, the possibility still remained that a specifically Christian initiation might subsist at its core for an elite that could not restrict itself to the narrowly exoteric point of view or enclose itself in such inherent limitations; but this is yet another question that we shall have to examine later.

Meanwhile, it should be noted that this change in the essential character—one might even say the very nature—of Christianity, explains perfectly what we mentioned at the outset: that everything preceding it was intentionally enveloped in obscurity, and even that it could not have been otherwise. Indeed, it is evident that insofar as it was essentially esoteric and initiatic, the nature of original Christianity would thus remain entirely hidden to those now admitted into a Christianity that had become exoteric; consequently, anything that might lead to a knowledge or even a suspicion of what Christianity was at its beginning had to be concealed by an impenetrable veil. We need not inquire as to the means by which such a result was obtained, which would rather be the business of historians if ever it occurred to them to ask such a question, a question that would in any case seem to them virtually insoluble since it is not one to which they could apply their habitual methodological reliance on 'documents' (which obviously could not exist in such a case); but what interests us here is only to establish the fact and to understand its true reason. We will add in this connection, however, that contrary to what those who are devotees of superficial and 'simplistic' rational explanations might think, this 'obscuration' can in no way

be attributed to ignorance, for it is all too evident that such ignorance could not have existed among those who must have been all
the more conscious of the transformation for having been more or
less directly involved in it. Neither can we claim, in accordance with
a prejudice widespread among those moderns who are only too
willing to lend their own mentality to others, that selfish and
'political' manoeuvres must have been involved, from which, in
any case, we cannot see what benefit could have accrued. On the
contrary, the truth is that this was strictly required by the very
nature of things in order to maintain the profound distinction
between the exoteric and esoteric domains, in conformity with
traditional orthodoxy.[11]

Some may perhaps ask what happened to the teachings of Christ
in consequence of such a change, since these teachings constitute by
definition the foundation of Christianity, from which foundation it
could not stray without ceasing to merit its name, not to mention
the difficulty of seeing what could be substituted for these teachings
without compromising the 'non-human' character without which
there is no longer any authentic tradition. In reality, these teachings
have been in no way touched or modified in their 'literalness' by
these events, and the permanence of the Gospel texts and other
writings of the New Testament, which obviously date from the earliest period of Christianity, provide sufficient proof of this.[12] What
changed was only the way they were understood, or, if one prefers,
the perspective from which they were envisaged and the resulting

11. We have pointed out elsewhere that the confusion between exoterism and
esoterism is one of the causes that most frequently gives rise to heterodox 'sects',
and there is in fact no doubt that this was the sole origin of some of the ancient
Christian heresies. This explains all the better the precautions taken to avoid this
confusion as much as possible, and their efficacy cannot be doubted in this regard
even though, from a different point of view, one is tempted to regret that their secondary effect was to bring almost insurmountable difficulties to any profound and
complete study of Christianity.

12. Even if one accepted—which we do not—the alleged conclusions of modern
'criticism', when the latter, with intentions only too manifestly anti-traditional,
seeks to assign these writings the most recent possible dates, these dates would certainly still be anterior to the transformation of which we are speaking.

significance that was accorded them. This is not to suggest, however, that there was anything false or illegitimate in this new understanding, for it goes without saying that the same truths are susceptible of application in different domains by virtue of the correspondences obtaining between all orders of reality. It is only to say that there are some precepts of special concern to those following an initiatic way and that are consequently applicable in a restricted and in some ways qualitatively homogeneous milieu, but which become impracticable in fact if they are extended to human society in general. This is recognized quite explicitly when they are considered to be only 'counsels of perfection' to which no obligation attaches,[13] which amounts to saying that each is to follow the evangelical way not only in the measure of his personal capacity, which is self-evident, but also according to what is permitted by the contingent circumstances in which he finds himself; and this is indeed all that can reasonably be demanded of those who do not aim to surpass simple exoteric practice.[14] On the other hand, as to doctrine strictly speaking, if there are truths that can be understood both exoterically and esoterically according to their reference to different degrees of reality, there are others that pertain exclusively to esoterism and have no correspondence outside it, becoming, as we have already said, wholly incomprehensible when one tries to transfer them to the exoteric domain, and one must then confine oneself to expressing them purely and simply as 'dogmatic' pronouncements to which the least explanation can never be attached. It is these that properly constitute what are generally called the 'mysteries' of Christianity. Indeed, the very existence of these 'mysteries' would be altogether unjustifiable if the esoteric character of early Christianity were denied; if, however, we take it into account, they appear on the contrary as a

13. We do not intend to speak of the abuses to which this sort of restriction or 'minimization' has sometimes given rise, but rather of the real need to adapt these precepts to a society composed of individuals as different and unequal as can be in respect of their spiritual level, but who must nevertheless be addressed by an exoterism in the same way and without exception.

14. This exoteric practice could be defined as the minimum necessary and sufficient to assure 'salvation', for that is indeed the sole aim it is in fact meant to achieve.

13

normal and inevitable consequence of the 'exteriorization' by which Christianity became the exoteric and specifically religious tradition we know today, even while preserving in appearance the same form in its doctrine and rites.

✠

Among the Christian rites, or more precisely among the sacraments that constitute their most essential part, those which present the greatest similarity to the rites of initiation and which consequently must be regarded as 'exteriorizations' of these latter—if in fact these had such a character in the beginning[15]—are as we have noted elsewhere naturally those that can be received only once, especially baptism. As long as the Christian community remained an initiatic organization, baptism, by which the neophyte was admitted into that community and in a sense 'incorporated' into it, evidently constituted the first initiation, which is to say the beginning of the 'lesser mysteries'. Moreover, this is clearly what is indicated by the character of 'second birth', which baptism preserved, although with a different application, even as it descended into the exoteric domain. So as not to have to come back to it let us immediately add that the rite of confirmation seems to have marked an accession to a higher degree, and it is most probable that this corresponded in principle to the completion of the 'lesser mysteries'. As for ordination, which now confers only the possibility of exercising certain functions, it can only be the 'exteriorization' of a sacerdotal initiation, pertaining as such to the 'greater mysteries'.

In order to realize that in what might be called the second state of Christianity the sacraments no longer retain any initiatic character and are really only exoteric rites, one need only consider the case of

---

15. In speaking here of 'rites of initiation' we mean those rites of which the actual aim is to communicate the initiatic influence; it goes without saying that apart from these there may exist other initiatic rites reserved for an elite that has already received initiation: one might suppose for example that the Eucharist was originally an initiatic rite in this sense, but not a rite of initiation.

14

baptism, since all the rest depend directly upon it. Despite the 'obscuration' of which we have spoken, we do at least know that at the very beginning rigorous precautions surrounded the conferring of baptism, and that those who were to receive it were subject to a long preparation. Today quite the reverse is the case, and it seems that everything possible has been done to facilitate to an extreme the reception of this sacrament, since not only is it conferred indiscriminately on one and all without question of qualification and preparation, but it can even be conferred validly by anyone at all, whereas the other sacraments may only be administered by priests or bishops, who exercise a definite ritual function. This easy attitude, coupled with the fact that infants are baptized as soon as possible after birth (which obviously excludes the idea of any sort of preparation whatsoever) can only be explained by a radical change in the very concept of baptism, a change following which it was considered to be an indispensable condition of 'salvation' and had consequently to be made available to the greatest possible number of individuals, whereas originally it was something altogether different. This way of envisaging things, by which 'salvation', the ultimate goal of all exoteric rites, is necessarily bound up with admission into the Christian church, is in short merely a result of the sort of 'exclusivism' that inevitably inheres in any exoterism as such. We do not think it useful to insist further on this, for it is only too clear that a rite conferred upon new-born infants, without any means being employed to determine their qualifications, could not have the character and value of an initiation, even if this were to be reduced to a mere virtuality. We shall, however, return in due course to the question whether a virtual initiation through the Christian sacraments remains possible.

We should make one additional point which is not without importance: in Christianity as it exists today, that is, in contrast to its original state, all rites without exception are public; everyone may be present at these rites, even at those which would have seemed to demand 'restriction', such as the ordination of a priest, the consecration of a bishop, or, with all the more reason, baptism or confirmation. Now this would be inadmissible in the case of rites of initiation, which normally can only be accomplished in the presence of those who have received the same initiation;[16] there is an obvious incompatibility between what is public, on the one hand, and the esoteric or initiatic on the other. If, however, we regard this argument as merely secondary, it is because one could claim that in the absence of other arguments it might imply no more than an abuse due to a certain degeneration that can appear from time to time in initiatic organizations without thereby depriving them of their intrinsic character. But we have seen quite clearly that the descent of Christianity into the exoteric order must not be considered a degeneration, and besides, the other reasons we give suffice to show that in this case there can really no longer be any question of initiation.

If Christianity still possessed a virtual initiation, as some have envisaged in their objections, and if in consequence those receiving the Christian sacraments, even baptism alone, no longer needed to seek any other form of initiation whatsoever,[17] how could one explain the specifically Christian initiatic organizations that incontestably existed throughout the Middle Ages, and what could have been their raison d'être if their particular rites were in a sense useless repetitions of the ordinary Christian rites? It will be said that these were only initiations into the 'lesser mysteries', so that those who wished to go further and gain access to the 'greater mysteries' would have had to seek another initiation; but apart from the fact that it is very unlikely, to say the least, that all who entered these organizations were prepared to approach that domain, there stands as a decisive fact against such a supposition the existence of Chris-

16. Following the article on Buddhist ordination mentioned earlier, we asked A.K. Coomaraswamy a question on this subject; he confirmed that this ordination was never conferred save in the presence of members of the *Sangha*, composed solely of those who had received it themselves, and excluding not only non-Buddhists, but also 'lay' adherents, who were basically only associates 'from outside'.

17. We are very much afraid that for many this may be the principal motive that persuades them that the Christian rites have preserved an initiatic value; they would in truth wish to dispense with all regular initiatic ties and yet be in a position to claim results in this order, and even if they admit that these results can only be exceptional under present conditions, each readily believes himself destined to be among the exceptions. It goes without saying that this is nothing more than a deplorable illusion.

tian Hermeticism, for by definition Hermeticism depends precisely on the 'lesser mysteries'—not to mention the craft initiations, which also belong to this same domain and which even in cases that cannot be called specifically Christian still required of their members in the Christian milieu the practice of the corresponding exoterism.

We must now anticipate another equivocation, for some may be tempted to draw from this an erroneous conclusion, thinking that if the sacraments no longer possess any initiatic quality they can have no initiatic effect, against which they would undoubtedly not fail to cite certain cases where the contrary seems to hold. The truth is that the sacraments cannot indeed have such effects by themselves, since their own efficacy is limited to the exoteric domain; but there is another thing to consider in this regard. Wherever there exist initiations that depend on one particular traditional form and that take its very exoterism as foundation, the exoteric rites can, in a certain way, be transposed into another order in the sense that they will serve as a support for the initiatic work itself and that consequently their effects will no longer be limited to the exoteric order, as is the case for the generality of the adherents of the same traditional form. In this respect Christianity is no different from other traditions, since there is, or was, a properly Christian initiation; only it must be understood that this initiatic use of the exoteric rites, far from dispensing with the need for regular initiation or taking its place, essentially presupposes it as the one necessary condition, a condition that could not be replaced even by the most exceptional qualifications, and without which everything that surpasses the ordinary level can at most only lead to mysticism, that is, to something that in reality still belongs to religious exoterism.

From what we have just said, it is easy to understand how it really was with those individuals in the Middle Ages who left writings manifestly initiatic in inspiration, and who today are wrongly taken for 'mystics' simply because nothing else is now known, but who were certainly something entirely different. It is not to be supposed that these were cases of 'spontaneous' initiation, or exceptional cases in which a virtual initiation that had remained attached to the sacraments might have become effective, at least not while there was still every possibility of a normal connection with one of the regular initiatic organizations that existed at that time, often under the cover of religious orders and even within them although not in any way a part of them. We cannot elaborate further on this since it would prolong the exposition indefinitely, but we will point out that it was precisely when these initiations ceased to exist, or at least ceased to be sufficiently accessible to offer real possibilities of an initiatic attachment, that mysticism properly speaking was born, so that the two things appear closely linked.[18] What we are saying here applies moreover only to the Roman Catholic church, and what is very remarkable too is that in the Eastern churches there has never been a 'mysticism' as understood in Western Christianity since the sixteenth century. This fact might lead us to think that a certain initiation of the kind we have just mentioned must have been maintained in those churches; and this is indeed what we find in hesychasm, of which the truly initiatic character seems indisputable, even if, as in so many other cases, it has been more or less diminished in modern times as a natural consequence of the general conditions of the age, conditions from which initiations can only escape by being very little known, either because they have always been so or because they have simply decided to 'close' themselves more than ever in order to avoid degeneration. In hesychasm, initiation in the strict sense consists essentially in the regular transmission of certain formulas, exactly comparable to the transmission of *mantras* in the Hindu tradition and of the *wird* in the Islamic *ṭuruq*. It also contains a complete 'technique' of invocation as a true method of interior work,[19] a method quite distinct from the exoteric Christian rites, although such a practice can nonetheless find a support in them as we explained, once the required formulas and the influence for which they are a vehicle have been validly transmitted, something

18. We do not wish to suggest that no forms of Christian initiation persisted after this, for we have reason to believe that something still remains of them even today, though in circumstances so restricted that they must in fact be considered as practically inaccessible, or else, as we shall see, in branches of Christianity other than the Roman Catholic church.

19. An interesting point in this regard is that such invocation is designated in Greek by the term *mnēmē*, 'memory' or 'remembrance', which is here the exact equivalent of the Arabic *dhikr*.

that naturally implies the existence of an uninterrupted initiatic chain since it is obvious that one can only transmit what one has oneself received.[20] These again are questions which we can only note summarily, but given that hesychasm still survives in our time, it seems to us that it would be possible to find in that direction some clarification about the nature and methods of other Christian initiations that belong, unfortunately, to the past.

In conclusion, we can say that despite its initiatic origins Christianity in its present state is certainly nothing more than a religion, that is, an exclusively exoteric tradition, and that it contains no possibilities other than those possessed by any other exoterism. Moreover, it makes no claim to more, because there is never a question of anything else but gaining 'salvation'. An initiation can naturally be superimposed upon it, and normally would even have to be, in order for the tradition to be truly complete, possessing effectively both esoteric and exoteric aspects; but this initiation does not currently exist in Christianity, at least in its Western form. It is in any case clear that observance of exoteric rites is fully sufficient for attaining 'salvation', and today more than ever that is all to which the great majority of human beings can legitimately aspire. But in such conditions, what are those individuals to do for whom, according to certain *mutaṣawwufīn*, 'Paradise is still nothing but a prison'?

---

20. It should be noted that among modern interpreters of hesychasm there are many who try to 'minimize' the importance of its properly 'technical' side, whether because that truly answers their tendencies, or because they think thus to free themselves from certain criticisms stemming from a total ignorance of initiatic matters; in either case we have here an example of the minimization we were speaking of earlier.

PART II

Some Christian
Initiatic Organizations

3

The Guardians
of the Holy Land

Among the functions of the Orders of Chivalry, particularly the Templars, one of the best known, though in general not the best understood, is that of 'Guardian of the Holy Land'. Certainly, if we restrict ourselves to the most outward meaning, we can find an immediate explanation of this fact in the connection between the origin of these orders and the Crusades, because, for Christians as for Jews, it does seem that the 'Holy Land' designates nothing other than Palestine. The question becomes more complicated, however, when we notice that various Eastern organizations of which the initiatic character cannot be doubted, such as the Assassins and the Druse, also took this same title of 'Guardians of the Holy Land'. In such cases it can certainly no longer be only a question of Palestine; and it is moreover remarkable that these organizations share a fairly large number of features with the Western Orders of Chivalry and that in certain cases there was even communication between them historically. What then ought we really to understand by the 'Holy Land', and to what exactly corresponds this role of 'guardian', which seems to be attached to a specific kind of initiation that might be called 'chivalric', giving the term a wider sense than usual but which the analogies that exist between the different forms in question will fully justify?

We have shown elsewhere, particularly in *The King of the World*, that the expression 'Holy Land' has several synonyms ('Pure Land', 'Land of the Saints', 'Land of the Blessed', 'Land of the Living', 'Land of Immortality'), and that these equivalent designations are found in the traditions of all peoples and always apply essentially to a spiritual center whose location in a given region may be understood either literally or symbolically, or sometimes in both senses at once. Every 'Holy Land' can be further designated by such expressions as 'Center of the World' or 'Heart of the World', something that calls for explanation since even such uniform terminology, when used in such different senses, could easily lead to confusion.

If, for example, we consider the Hebraic tradition, we see that the *Sepher Yetsirah* speaks of the 'Holy Palace' or 'Interior Palace', which is the true 'Center of the World' in the cosmogonic sense of the term; and we see also that this 'Holy Palace' has its image in the human world in that the *Shekinah*—the 'real presence' of the Divinity— abides in a specific place.[1] For the Israelites, this abode of the *Shekinah* was the Tabernacle (*Mishkan*), which in consequence they considered to be the 'Heart of the World', for it was indeed the spiritual center of their own tradition. This center, moreover, did not at first have a fixed location, since the spiritual center of a nomadic people, as they were, must necessarily move with them while nevertheless always remaining the same. 'The abode of the *Shekinah*,' says Paul Vulliaud, 'was not fixed until the completion of the Temple, for which David had provided Solomon the gold and silver and everything else necessary to perfect the work.[2] The Tabernacle of the Holiness of *Jehovah*, the abode of the *Shekinah*, is the Holy of Holies that forms the heart of the Temple, which is itself the center of Zion (Jerusalem), just as Holy Zion is the center of the Land of Israel, and the Land of Israel is the Center of the World.'[3] In these successive applications we notice a gradual extension of the idea of the center, so that the appellation 'Center of the World' or 'Heart of the World' is finally extended to the entire land of Israel insofar as this is regarded as the 'Holy Land'; and it should be added

1. See our articles 'Le Coeur du Monde dans la Kabbale hébraïque' and 'La Terre Sainte et le Coeur du Monde' in the journal *Regnabit*, July–August and September– October 1926. Cf. also chap. 4 of *The Symbolism of the Cross*.

2. It is fitting to note that the expressions used here evoke the assimilation often made between the construction of the Temple, envisaged in terms of its ideal mean- ing, and the 'Great Work' of the Hermeticists.

3. *La Kabbale juive*, Paris, 1923, p509.

in this connection that it has still other designations, among them 'Land of the Living'. One speaks of the 'Land of the Living comprising seven lands', and Vulliaud observes that 'this land is Canaan, in which there were seven nations,'[4] which is correct in its literal sense although a symbolic interpretation is equally possible. This expression 'Land of the Living' is exactly synonymous with 'abode of immortality', and Catholic liturgy applies it to the celestial abode of the elect, which the Promised Land in fact symbolized, since upon entering it Israel was to reach the end of all its tribulations. From yet another point of view, the land of Israel, as a spiritual center, was an image of heaven, for according to Judaic tradition 'all that the Israelites accomplish on earth is in accord with the patterns that unfold in the celestial world.'[5]

What has been said here of the Israelites may equally well be said of all peoples possessing a truly orthodox tradition; and in fact the nation of Israel is not the only one to have likened its country to the 'Heart of the World' and to have regarded it as an image of heaven, two ideas that are, after all, really one. This same symbolism is encountered among other peoples who also possessed a 'Holy Land', that is, a country where a spiritual center played a role comparable to that played by the Temple in Jerusalem for the Hebrews. In this respect the 'Holy Land' is like the *Omphalos*, which was always the visible image of the 'Center of the World' for the people inhabiting the region where it was situated.[6]

This symbolism is found especially among the ancient Egyptians. According to Plutarch, 'Egypt ... which has the blackest of soils, they call by the same name as the black portion of the eye, "Chemia",[7] and compare it to the heart.' The rather strange reason given by the author is that 'it is warm and moist and is enclosed by

---

4. Ibid., vol. 2, p 116.

5. Ibid., vol. 1, p 501.

6. See our article 'Thunderbolts', in *Symbols of Sacred Science*, chap. 27.

7. In the Egyptian language *kemi* signifies 'black earth', a designation for which equivalents can also be found among other peoples; from this word comes 'alchemy' (*al* merely being the article in Arabic), which originally designated the Hermetic science, that is, the sacerdotal science of Egypt.

the southern portions of the inhabited world and adjoins them, like the heart in a man's left side,'[8] for 'the Egyptians believe the eastern regions are the face of the world, the northern the right, and the southern the left.'[9] These correspondences are rather superficial, and the true reason must be quite different since the same comparison with the heart has been applied likewise to every land to which a sacred and spiritually 'central' character has been attributed, no matter what its geographical situation. Moreover, according to Plutarch himself, the heart, which represented Egypt, at the same time represented heaven: 'And the heavens, since they are ageless because of their eternity, they portray by a heart with a censer beneath it.'[10] And so, whereas the heart is itself figured as a vase, which is none other than what the legends of the Western Middle Ages were to call the 'Holy Grail', it functions in turn and simultaneously as hieroglyph both for Egypt and for heaven.

The conclusion to be drawn from these considerations is that there are as many particular 'Holy Lands' as there are regular traditional forms, since they represent the spiritual centers that correspond respectively to these different forms; however, if the same symbolism applies uniformly to all these 'Holy Lands', it is because all these spiritual centers have an analogous constitution, often extending to the most precise details, inasmuch as they are all images of the same unique and supreme center that alone is truly the 'Center of the World', from which they take their attributes as participating in its nature by direct communication (which is what constitutes traditional orthodoxy), and as effectively representing it more or less outwardly for particular times and places. In other

8. 'Isis and Osiris', in *Plutarch, Moralia*, vol. v., tr. Frank Cole Babbitt (Cambridge: Harvard University Press, 1936), par. 33, p 83. ED.

9. Ibid., par. 32, p 79. In India on the contrary it is the South that is designated as the 'right side' (*dakshina*); but despite appearances this comes to the same thing, for this should be understood as the side to one's right when facing the East, while on the other hand it is easy to visualize the left side of the world as extending to the right of the person contemplating it, and conversely—as happens for two persons facing each other.

10. Ibid., par. 10, p 27. This symbol, with the significance it is given here, seems susceptible of comparison with that of the phoenix.

words, there exists one 'Holy Land' par excellence, the prototype of all the others and the spiritual center to which all other centers are subordinate, the seat of the primordial tradition from which all the particular traditions are derived by adaptation to whatever specific conditions attach to a people or an epoch. This 'Holy Land' par excellence is the 'supreme country', according to the meaning of the Sanskrit term *Paradesha,* from which the Chaldeans made *Pardes* and Westerners *Paradise*; it is indeed the 'Terrestrial Paradise', which is the starting-point of every tradition, having at its center the unique source from which the four rivers flow to the four cardinal points,[11] and which is also the 'abode of immortality', as can easily be seen by turning to the first chapters of Genesis.[12]

We cannot think of returning here to all the questions concerning the supreme center and which we have already treated more or less amply elsewhere: its preservation, with varying degrees of secrecy, according to the period concerned, from the beginning to the end of the cycle, that is from the 'Terrestrial Paradise' to the 'Celestial Jerusalem', which represent its two extremes; the many names by which it has been known, among them *Tula, Luz, Salem,* and *Agarttha*; and the different symbols that have represented it, such as the mountain, the cavern, the island, and many more, standing for the most part in direct relation to the symbolism of the 'Pole' or the 'World Axis'. To these representations we may also add those which make of it a city, a citadel, a temple, or a palace, according to the particular aspect under which it is envisaged; and this gives us occasion to recall not only the Temple of Solomon, which relates more directly to our subject, but also the triple enclosure, of which we wrote recently that it represents the initiatic

11. This source is identical with the 'fountain of teaching' to which we have had occasion to make various allusions (see below).

12. This is why the 'fountain of teaching' is at the same time the 'fountain of youth' (*fons juventutis*), for whoever drinks of it is freed from the temporal condition; it is moreover situated at the foot of the 'Tree of Life' (see the following two-part study 'The Secret Language of Dante and the Fedeli d'Amore'), and its waters are obviously identified with the 'elixir of longevity' of the Hermeticists (the idea of 'longevity' having here the same significance as in the Eastern traditions) or the 'draught of immortality' so often encountered under various names.

hierarchy of certain traditional centers,[13] and also the mysterious labyrinth, which, though in a more complex form, pertains to a similar conception, with the difference that it emphasizes above all the idea of a 'journey' to the hidden center.[14]

We must now add that the symbolism of the 'Holy Land' has a double meaning: whether it be related to the supreme center or to a subordinate center, it represents not only that center itself, but also, by natural association, the tradition emanating from the former or conserved by the latter, that is, in the first case, the primordial tradition, and in the second, a particular traditional form.[15] This double meaning appears again clearly in the symbolism of the 'Holy Grail', which is at once a vessel (*grasale*) and a book (*gradale* or *graduale*), the latter manifestly designating the tradition, while the former more directly pertains to the state corresponding to the effective possession of this tradition, that is, the 'edenic state', if it is the primordial tradition that is being considered, for whoever has attained this state is thereby reintegrated into *Pardes*, so that one can say his abode is henceforth in the 'Center of the World'.[16] It is not without reason that we bring these two symbolisms together here, for their

13. See our article 'The Triple Enclosure of the Druids', *Symbols of Sacred Science*, chap. 12, where we point out the precise relationship of that figure in both its circular and its square forms with the symbolism of the 'Terrestrial Paradise' and the 'Celestial Jerusalem'.

14. The Cretan labyrinth was the palace of Minos, whose name, identical with that of Manu, designates the primordial Legislator. It is evident, moreover, from the point we are making, why walking the labyrinths traced upon the paving stones of certain churches in the Middle Ages was considered to replace the pilgrimage to the Holy Land for those who were unable to accomplish it; and it should be remembered that pilgrimage is precisely one of the figures of initiation, so that 'pilgrimage to the Holy Land' is, in the esoteric sense, the same thing as the 'search for the Lost Word' or the 'quest for the Holy Grail'.

15. By analogy, the 'Center of the World' is, from the cosmogonic viewpoint, the original point from which the creative Word is uttered, and is also the Word itself.

16. It is important to remember here that in all traditions places essentially symbolize states. We would point out further that there is an obvious connection between the symbolism of the vase or cup and that of the fountain mentioned earlier. We have also seen that for the Egyptians the vase was the hieroglyph of the heart, the vital center of the being. And finally, let us recall what we have already

28

very close similarity shows that when we speak of the 'Knighthood of the Holy Grail' or of the 'Guardians of the Holy Land' we must understand one and the same thing. It remains, then, for us to explain as far as is possible just what the function of these 'guardians' was, a function that fell particularly to the Templars.[17]

In order to understand clearly what is involved here, a distinction must be made between the custodians of the tradition, whose duty is to conserve and transmit it, and those who to one degree or another only receive from it a communication and, one might say, a participation. The original trustees and dispensers of the doctrine remain at its source, which is strictly the center itself; thence the doctrine is communicated and distributed hierarchically to the different initiatic degrees in accordance with the currents represented by the rivers of *Pardes*, or, recalling a figure we have examined elsewhere,[18] by the channels running from the interior to the exterior, linking together the successive enclosures that correspond to these degrees. Thus not all who share in the tradition reach the same degree or fulfill the same function; and a distinction should even be made between these two things, for although in general they correspond to each other, they are not strictly inseparable, for it can happen that a man may be intellectually qualified to attain the highest degrees but is not thereby qualified to discharge all the functions in the initiatic organization. Here only the functions are under consideration, and from this point of view we would say that the 'guardians' stand at the boundary of the spiritual center, taken in its widest sense, or in the uttermost enclosure, which both separates the center from the 'outer world' and brings it into contact with the latter. Thus, these 'guardians' exercise a double function: on the one hand, they are truly the defenders of the 'Holy Land' in the sense that they

---

said on other occasions about wine as a substitute for the Vedic *soma* and as symbol of the hidden doctrine; in all of this, in one way or another, it is always a matter of the 'draught of immortality' and the restoration of the 'primordial state'.

17. Saint-Yves d'Alveydre refers to the 'guardians' of the supreme center as 'Templars of the Agarttha'; the observations we have made make clear the aptness of this expression, the full significance of which he perhaps did not fully grasp himself.

18. See 'The Triple Enclosure of the Druids', *Symbols of Sacred Science*, chap. 12.

bar access to those not possessing the qualifications required for entry, and constitute what we have called the 'outer covering' that conceals it from the eyes of the profane; on the other hand, however, they assure regular relations with the outside world, as we shall explain.

In the language of the Hindu tradition the role of defender clearly belongs to the Kshatriyas, and it is precisely 'chivalric' initiation that is essentially adapted to the nature proper to the men of this warrior caste. From this derive the special features of this initiation, the particular symbolism it uses, and especially the intervention of an affective element designated very explicitly by the term 'love', something we have already explained elsewhere and cannot pause to consider now.[19] But in the case of the Templars there is something more to keep in mind: although their initiation was essentially 'chivalric', as was appropriate to their nature and function, they had a double character, at once military and religious; and it had to be so if they were, as we have good reason to think, among the 'guardians' of the supreme center, where spiritual authority and temporal power are brought together in their common principle, communicating the mark of that reunion in turn to all things directly connected with it. In the Western world, where the spiritual takes a specifically religious form, the true 'guardians of the Holy Land', as long as they had any 'official' existence, had to be knights, but knights who were at the same time monks; and that indeed is just what the Templars were.

This brings us directly to the second role of the 'guardians' of the supreme center, a role that consists, as we have just said, in assuring certain exterior relations and above all, let us add, in maintaining the link between the primordial tradition and the secondary, derived traditions. To this end each traditional form must possess one or more special organizations constituted, to all appearances, within that form itself, but composed of men aware of what lies beyond all 'forms', that is to say of the one doctrine that is the source and essence of all the others, and that is none other than the primordial tradition. In the world of the Judeo-Christian tradition

19. See below, chap. 5: 'The Secret Language of Dante and the Fedeli d'Amore'.

such an organization naturally enough took as its symbol the Temple of Solomon, which had long since ceased to exist physically and could thus have only an altogether ideal significance as a reflection (as is every subordinate spiritual center) of the supreme center; and the very etymology of the name Jerusalem quite clearly indicates that it is only the visible image of the mysterious *Salem* of Melchizedek. If such was the nature of the Templars, in order to fulfill the role allotted them and which concerned a certain specific tradition, that of the West, they had to remain outwardly attached to the form of that tradition; but at the same time the inner consciousness of the true doctrinal unity must have enabled them to communicate with the representatives of other traditions,[20] which explains their relations with certain Eastern organizations, especially, as is only natural, with those who furthermore played a role similar to their own.

These considerations make it clear on the other hand why the destruction of the Order of the Temple[21] should have brought in its wake the rupture of regular relations between the West and the 'Center of the World'; and the deviation that inevitably followed this rupture and that has become gradually more marked since then up to our own time must indeed be traced back to the fourteenth century. This is not to say however that all ties were severed at one blow; for quite some time it was possible to maintain relations with the supreme center to some degree, though only covertly, through the mediation of such organizations as the *Fede Santa*[22] or the Fedeli d'Amore,[23] the *Massenie du Saint-Graal*, and doubtless many others also heir to the spirit of the Order of the Temple and for the most part attached to it by more or less direct filiation. Those who preserved this spirit alive and who inspired such organi-

20. This relates to what has been called symbolically the 'gift of tongues'; on this subject we would refer readers to the study of the same name [chap. 37] in *Perspectives on Initiation*.

21. Guénon usually prefers this full designation for the Knights Templars. ED.

22. A tertiary order of the Templars. ED.

23. The 'Faithful of Love', of which Guénon will speak further in this text. The Italian spelling for this association has been used throughout in preference to the French *Fedèles d'Amour*. ED.

zations, though without themselves constituting a formal group, came to be known by the essentially symbolic name 'brothers of the Rose-Cross'; but a day came when even these brothers of the Rose-Cross had to leave the West, where conditions had become such that no further action was possible; and so, it is said, they withdrew to Asia, reabsorbed as it were by the supreme center of which they were a kind of emanation. For the Western world there is no longer a 'Holy Land' to guard, since the path leading to it was from that moment utterly lost. How much longer will this situation endure, and is it even to be hoped that communication might be re-established sooner or later? It is not for us to answer this question, for apart from the fact that we do not wish to risk any prediction, the solution depends entirely upon the West itself, for only by a return to normal conditions and a recovery of the spirit of its own tradition will it prove able to open anew the way that leads to the 'Center of the World'.

4

The Secret Language
of Dante and the
'Fedeli d'Amore' [1]

Under the title *Il linguaggio segreto di Dante a dei fidele d'amore*,[1] Luigi Valli, to whom we are already indebted for several studies on the significance of Dante's writings, has published a new work that is too important for us to pass by with no more than a mere bibliographical note. Its thesis may be briefly summarized as follows: the various 'ladies' celebrated by the poets attached to the mysterious organization of the Fedeli d'Amore, from Dante, Guido Cavalcanti, and their contemporaries, to Boccaccio and Petrarch, are not women who actually lived on this earth but are all, under different names, one and the same symbolic 'Lady', who represents transcendent Intelligence (the *Madonna Intelligenza* of Dino Compagni) or divine Wisdom. In support of this thesis the author brings forward formidable documentation and a collection of arguments that must impress even the most sceptical; in particular he shows that those verses that seem most unintelligible from the literal point of view become perfectly clear with the hypothesis of a 'jargon' or conventional language the principal terms of which he claims to have interpreted; and he recalls other cases, notably that of the Persian Sufis, where a similar meaning has been concealed in this fashion under the guise of simple love poetry. It would not be feasible to summarize his whole argument, which is based on exact textual citations that support his views, and so we can only refer anyone interested in the subject to the book itself.

1. Roma: Biblioteca di filosofia e Scienza, Casa éditrice 'Optima', 1928.

33

In truth, what is involved has always seemed to us an obvious and incontestable fact, though one nevertheless needing to be firmly established. Indeed, Valli foresees that his conclusions will be challenged by several kinds of adversary: firstly, the so-called 'positivist' criticism (which he is wrong to qualify as 'traditional' since it is, on the contrary, opposed to the traditional spirit, to which all initiatic interpretation is linked); secondly, the party spirit, whether Catholic or anti-Catholic, which will find no satisfaction at all in what he writes; and finally, 'aesthetic' criticism and 'romantic rhetoric', which are fundamentally nothing other than what one might call the 'literary' spirit. We have here a group of prejudices that will always and inevitably stand opposed to the search for the profound meaning of certain works, though in the presence of such works those of good faith and open mind will readily see which side the truth is on. For our part, the only objections we have to make concern certain interpretations that in no way affect the general thesis; moreover, the author has made no claim to provide a definitive solution to all the questions he raises and is the first to acknowledge that his work will require correction or amendment in many points of detail.

Valli's principal shortcoming, whence stem most of the insufficiencies observed in his work, is—let us say it plainly—that he lacks the 'initiatic' mentality required to treat such a subject in depth. His point of view is too exclusively that of an historian: it is not enough to 'investigate history' in order to solve certain problems; and, moreover, we are entitled to wonder whether this does not really amount to interpreting medieval ideas with the modern mentality, a reproach the author quite rightly levels at the official critics. Did the men of the Middle Ages ever 'investigate history for its own sake'? The above matters require a more profound kind of understanding, and if one brings to them only a 'profane' spirit and intention, one can only accumulate materials reflecting an altogether different spirit; and we do not see that there could be much interest in historical research if some doctrinal truth does not result from it.

It is truly regrettable that the author lacks certain traditional data and a direct and so to speak 'technical' knowledge of his subject-matter. This prevented him from recognizing the properly initiatic import of our study *The Esoterism of Dante* and explains why he did not understand how little it matters, from our point of view, whether such 'discoveries' be attributed to Rossetti, Aroux, or to anyone else, for we cite them only as 'supports' for considerations of quite another order: we are concerned with initiatic doctrine, not literary history. As regards Rossetti, we find rather strange the asser-tion that he was 'Rosicrucian' since the true brothers of the Rose-Cross (who were, by the way, not of 'Gnostic descent') had disap-peared from the Western world well before his time; and even if he were attached to some sort of pseudo-Rosicrucian organization, of which there were so many, such an organization would certainly not have had any authentic tradition to impart to him. Moreover, Ros-setti's initial idea of reading a purely political meaning into every-thing quite clearly contradicts such an hypothesis. Valli has only a very superficial and altogether 'simplistic' idea of Rosicrucianism, and he does not seem to have any inkling of the symbolism of the cross any more than he seems to have understood the traditional significance of the heart, which refers to the intellect and not to feelings. Let us say on this last point that the *cuore gentile* of the 'Fidèles d'Amore' is the heart purified, that is, devoid of all that concerns worldly objects, and by this very fact made ready to receive interior illumination. It is remarkable that an identical doctrine is found in Taoism.

Let us move on to some other points raised in the course of our reading, for there are some rather unfortunate references that detract from this otherwise serious work. Thus one might easily have found better authorities to cite on Gnosticism than G.R.S. Mead,[2] on number symbolism than Marc Saunier, and above all on Masonry than Léo Taxil![3] Moreover, Valli cites the last mentioned on

---

2. G.R.S. Mead was a classical scholar and indefatigable translator of important and often obscure Gnostic and Hermetic texts, who allied his work for a time with the Theosophical Movement of H.P. Blavatsky. ED.

3. Léo Taxil was a pseudonym of Gabriel Jogand-Pagès, a controversial figure who was prosecuted several times for unscrupulous journalism, and who was at one time a virulent anti-cleric and active Mason. He subsequently perpetrated an elaborate anti-Masonic hoax, for which he achieved great notoriety. Taxil, ever diff-icult to pin down, would at one time claim that his motive had been to destroy Freemasonry by associating it with satanic practices, and then again imply that he only wanted to see how credulous the Catholic church could be! ED.

a most elementary point, the symbolic ages of the different grades, something that can be found anywhere. In the same place, following Rossetti, the author also cites the *Recueil precieux de la Maçonnerie Adonhiramite*; but the reference is made in an altogether unintelligible fashion, which clearly demonstrates that he himself has no personal knowledge of the book in question. We have, besides, grave reservations concerning everything Valli says of Masonry, which he qualifies bizarrely as 'ultra-modern'; an organization may have 'lost the spirit' (or what is called in Arabic the *barakah*) through the intrusion of politics or otherwise, yet keep its symbolism intact even while no longer understanding it; but Valli himself seems not to have a very good grasp of the true role of symbolism nor a very clear sense of traditional filiation. When he speaks of the different 'currents' he confuses esoterism and exoterism and takes as sources of inspiration for the Fedeli d'Amore what only represent prior incursions into the profane world of an initiatic tradition from which these Fedeli d'Amore themselves proceeded directly. Influences descend from the initiatic sphere into the profane world, but the inverse is not possible, for a river never returns to its source; that source is the 'fountain of teaching' so often in evidence in the poems studied here, and generally described as situated at the foot of a tree that is obviously none other than the 'Tree of Life'.[4] The symbolism of the 'Terrestrial Paradise' and of the 'Celestial Jerusalem' must find its application here.

There are also some no less regrettable linguistic inaccuracies: thus the author qualifies as 'human' things that are on the contrary essentially 'supra-human', as, moreover, is the case for anything of a truly traditional and initiatic order. Similarly, he commits the error of calling initiates of any grade whatever 'adepts',[5] whereas that term must be strictly reserved for the supreme degree. The misuse of this

4. This tree, among the Fedeli d'Amore, is generally a pine, a beech, or a laurel; the 'Tree of Life' is often represented by evergreens.

5. The Fedeli d'Amore were divided into seven degrees; these are the seven rungs of the initiatic ladder, corresponding to the seven planetary heavens and the seven liberal arts. The expressions 'terzo cielo' (heaven of Venus), 'terzo loco' (to be compared with the Masonic term 'third apartment'), and 'terzo grado' indicate the

word is particularly noteworthy because it constitutes, so to speak, a 'hallmark': there are a certain number of mistakes that the 'profane' rarely fail to commit, and this is one of them. We should also call attention to the constant use of words such as 'sect' and 'sectarian' to designate organizations that are initiatic and not religious, an entirely improper and most displeasing usage,[6] which brings us directly to the gravest shortcoming we must point out in Valli's work.

This failing is Valli's continual confusion of the 'initiatic' and the 'mystical' points of view, and his assimilation of the matters in question into a 'religious' doctrine, whereas esoterism, even if it bases itself on religious forms (as is the case with the Sufis and the Fedeli d'Amore), really belongs to an entirely different order. A truly initiatic tradition cannot be 'heterodox'; to qualify it as such is to reverse the normal and hierarchical relationship between the interior and the exterior. Esoterism is not contrary to 'orthodoxy', even orthodoxy construed simply in the religious sense; it is above or beyond the religious point of view, which is obviously not at all the same thing; and in fact the unjustified accusation of heresy was often nothing more than a convenient ruse for getting rid of people who might be problematic for altogether different reasons. Rossetti and Aroux were not wrong in thinking that in Dante's works theological expressions mask something else, but only in believing that these expressions must be interpreted 'inversely'; esoterism is not superimposed on exoterism, but neither is it opposed to it, for it is not on the same plane and gives to the same truths a deeper meaning by transposing them to a higher order. It is of course true that *Amor* is the inverse of *Roma*, but we must not conclude from that, as some

---

third degree of the hierarchy in which the *saluto* (or 'salute') was received, this rite taking place, it seems, at the feast of All Saints, as did others at Easter, around which the action of *The Divine Comedy* is centered.

6. This is not at all the same thing, whatever some may think, as 'jargon' (*gergo*), which, as we have pointed out (*Voile d'Isis*, Oct. 1926, p652), was a technical term before passing into popular usage, where it took on a pejorative sense. Let us point out here also that we always take the word 'profane' in its technical sense, which of course implies nothing insulting.

have wished to do, that it signifies the antithesis of *Roma*,[7] but rather that *Roma* is only its reflection or visible image, necessarily inverted as is the image of an object in a mirror—which gives us occasion to recall the *per speculum in aenigmate* of Saint Paul. Regarding Rossetti and Aroux and some reservations we have about certain of their interpretations, we will add that one cannot say a method is 'unacceptable because unverifiable' without running the risk of falling into the prejudices of 'positivist' criticism, which would entail rejecting everything obtained by direct knowledge, especially and in particular all knowledge obtained through the regular transmission of a traditional teaching, which is in effect unverifible... for the profane![8]

It is the more astonishing that Valli confuses esoterism with 'heterodoxy' in view of the fact that he has at least understood, far better than his predecessors, that the doctrine of the Fedeli d'Amore was in no way 'anti-Catholic' (even being, like that of the Rosicrucians, rigorously 'catholic' in the true sense of the word) and that it had nothing in common with the profane currents from which the Reformation was to come. Where then did he get the idea that the Church had revealed the deeper meaning of its 'mysteries' to the general populace? On the contrary, so little of this is taught by the Church that one comes to doubt, with good reason, whether she herself has retained any knowledge of it; and it is precisely in this 'loss of spirit' that the 'corruption' already denounced by Dante and his associates consisted,[9] although the most elementary prudence

---

7. It is curious that if one writes this simple phrase, 'In Italia è Roma' [In Italy and Rome], and then reads it backward, it becomes 'Amore ai Latini' [Love to the Latins]: 'chance' is sometimes surprisingly ingenious!

8. It must be admitted that it is difficult to avoid the influence of the spirit of the times; thus, the qualification of certain Biblical books as 'pseudo-solomonic' and 'mystico-platonic' seems to us an annoying concession to modern exegesis, that is to say to the same 'positivist criticism' against which the author so justifiably takes his stand.

9. The head of Medusa, which turns men to 'stone' (a word that plays a very important part in the language of the Fedeli d'Amore), represents the corruption of Wisdom; her hair (according to the Sufis symbolic of the divine mysteries) turns into serpents, naturally taken in the pejorative sense, for in its other sense the serpent is also a symbol of Wisdom itself.

dictated that when speaking of this 'corruption' they not do so clearly. But one should not conclude from this that the use of a symbolic terminology has no other raison d'être than the desire to conceal the true meaning of a doctrine; there are things that by their very nature cannot be expressed otherwise than in this form, and this side of the question, which is by far the most important, scarcely seems to have been recognized by the author. And there is yet a third aspect, intermediate so to speak, where prudence is indeed involved, but in the interest of the doctrine itself and no longer of its exponents. This aspect is more particularly related to the symbol of wine used by the Sufis, whose teaching, let us add in passing, cannot be qualified as 'pantheistic' except by a typical Western error. The allusions he makes to this symbol in no way establish that 'wine' signifies 'mystery', a secret or restricted doctrine, simply because *yayin* and *sôd* are equivalent numerically in Hebrew, or because in Islamic esoterism wine is the 'drink of the elite', which the common man may not use with impunity.[10]

But let us move on to the confusion of the 'mystical' with the 'initiatic' point of view, a confusion that is connected to the preceding one because it is the false assimilation of esoteric doctrines to mysticism (which latter pertains to the religious domain) that leads to situating them on the same plane as exoterism and insisting on

---

10. The proverbial expression 'to drink like a Templar', generally taken in the most crudely literal sense, doubtless has this as its real origin since the 'wine' that the Templars drank was the same as that drunk by the Jewish Kabbalists and the Islamic Sufis. Similarly, the other expression, 'to swear like a Templar', is only an allusion to the initiatic vow, robbed of its proper significance by profane incomprehension and malice. [To better understand what the author is saying in this text it should be noted that wine taken in the ordinary sense of the word is a forbidden beverage in Islam; hence, whenever reference is made to it in Islamic esoterism it must be understood to designate something more subtle. In fact, according to the teaching of Muḥyi'd-Dīn ibn al-'Arabī, 'wine' signifies the 'science of spiritual states' (*ilm al-aḥwāl*), whereas 'water' represents the 'absolute science' (*al-ilm al-mutlaq*), 'milk' the 'science of revealed laws' (*ilmu-ch-chrāy'i*), and 'honey' the 'science of sapiential norms' (*ilm al-nawamīs*). Moreover, if one notes that these four 'beverages' are precisely the substances of the four paradisal rivers according to the Koran (47, 17), it will be understood that the 'wine' of the Sufis differs in substance from the familiar beverage that serves as its symbol—and this applies to the other three initiatic beverages as well.—note by M.Valsan.]

39

opposing them to it. We see very well what it is in the present case that could have provoked this error: a 'chivalric' tradition always requires the preponderance of a principle represented as feminine (*Madonna*)[11] as well as the intervention of an affective element (*Amore*) in order to adapt to the nature of the men to whom it is particularly addressed. The linking of such a traditional form with that represented by the Persian Sufis is altogether sound, but it should be added that these two are far from being the only cases where one encounters the cult of the 'donna-Divinità', that is to say the feminine aspect of the Divinity: we also find it in India, where that aspect is designated as the *Shakti*, equivalent in certain respects to the Hebraic *Shekinah*; and it should be noted that the cult of the *Shakti* concerns above all the Kshatriyas. A 'chivalric' tradition is precisely nothing other than a traditional form appropriate to the Kshatriyas, and that is why it cannot constitute a path that is purely intellectual as is that of the Brahmins; the latter is the 'dry way' of the alchemists, whereas the former is the 'moist way',[12] water symbolizing the feminine as fire does the masculine, the first corresponding to the emotivity and the second to the intellectuality that predominate respectively in the natures of the Kshatriyas and the Brahmins. This is why such a tradition may seem mystical from the outside even when it is really initiatic, so much so that one could even think that mysticism in the ordinary sense of the word is a sort of vestige of it, a 'survival' in a civilization such as that of the West, after every regular traditional organization has disappeared.

The role of the feminine principle in certain traditional forms is noticeable even in Catholic exoterism in the importance attributed to the cult of the Virgin. Valli seems astonished to find the *Rosa Mys-*

11. The 'active Intellect', represented by *Madonna*, is the 'celestial ray' that constitutes the link between God and man, and that leads man to God: it is the Hindu *Buddhi*. Nevertheless, one should beware of taking 'Wisdom' and 'Intelligence' as strictly identical, for there are two complementary aspects to be distinguished here (*Hokmah* and *Binah* in the Kabbalah).

12. In another sense, and according to another correlation, these two ways might also be, respectively, that of initiates in general and that of mystics; but the latter way is 'irregular' and need not be envisaged by anyone holding strictly to the traditional norm.

tica figuring in the litanies of the Virgin, but there are in these same litanies many other properly initiatic symbols, and what he does not seem to suspect is that their application is perfectly justified through the association of the Virgin with Wisdom and with the *Shekinah*.[13] Apropos of this let us also note that Saint Bernard, whose connection with the Templars is well known, appears as a 'knight of the Virgin'; and he calls the Virgin 'his Lady', the origin of the expression 'Our Lady' [*Notre Dame*] even having been attributed to him. She is also *Madonna*, and in one of her aspects is identified with Wisdom, hence the same *Madonna* of the Fedeli d'Amore, this being yet another correspondence Valli does not suspect, any more than he seems to suspect the reason why the month of May is consecrated to the Virgin.

One thing ought to have led Valli to see that the doctrines in question were not 'mysticism' at all: he himself acknowledges the almost exclusive importance these doctrines attach to 'knowledge', something totally foreign to the mystical point of view. He is mistaken, moreover, about the consequences to be drawn therefrom, for this emphasis is not a characteristic peculiar to 'gnosticism', but a general feature of all initiatic teaching, whatever form it may have taken; knowledge is always the sole aim, and all the rest but different means of attaining it. One must take care not to confuse 'gnosis', which signifies 'knowledge', with 'gnosticism', although the latter obviously takes its name from the former; besides, the term 'gnosticism' is rather vague and seems in fact to have been applied indiscriminately to very different things.[14]

---

13. It should be noted that in certain cases the same symbols even represent simultaneously the Virgin and Christ. This is indeed an enigma worthy of being posed to the sagacity of our modern researchers, and its solution would result from a consideration of the links of the *Shekinah* with *Metatron*. [Cf. *The King of the World*, chap. 3].

14. Valli says that the 'critics' show little appreciation for the traditional theses of contemporary 'gnostics'; for once such 'critics' are in the right because these 'neo-gnostics' have never received anything through any transmission whatsoever, and all that is involved is an attempt at a 'reconstitution' from documents, very fragmentary ones, that lie within reach of one and all. On this point one can believe the testimony of someone who has had occasion to observe these things closely enough to know the real story.

One must not allow oneself to be hindered by external forms, of whatever kind they may be. The 'Fedeli d'Amore' were well able to go beyond these forms, as is attested by the fact that in one of the first tales of Boccaccio's *Decameron*, Melchizedek affirms that, as between Judaism, Christianity, and Islam, 'no one knows which is the true faith.' Valli was right to interpret this affirmation in the sense that 'the true faith lies hidden under the external aspects of the various beliefs,' but what is most remarkable here—and this he did not see—is that these words are put into the mouth of Melchizedek, who is precisely the representative of the single tradition concealed under all these outer forms, clearly indicating that certain individuals in the West at that time had retained a knowledge of the true 'Center of the World'. However that may be, an 'affective' language, such as that of the Fedeli d'Amore, is also an outer form by which one must not be fooled, for it may very well conceal something far more profound; and the word *amour* in particular may, by virtue of an analogical transposition, signify something altogether different from the sentiment it ordinarily denotes. This deeper meaning of 'love' in connection with the doctrines of the Orders of Chivalry becomes clear enough if one considers the following together: firstly, Saint John's phrase, 'God is Love'; then the battle-cry of the Templars, 'Vive Dieu, Saint Amour'; and finally the last verse of the *Divine Comedy*, 'L'Amor che muove il Sole e l'altre stelle.'[15] Another interesting point in this regard is the relationship established between 'love' and 'death' in the symbolism of the Fedeli d'Amore, a twofold relationship, as the word death itself has a double meaning. On the one hand, there is a parallel and a sort of association of love with death, where the latter must be understood as 'initiatic death'; and this parallel seems to have endured in the current that, at the close of the Middle Ages, gave rise to the depictions of the 'dance of death' [*danse macabre*];[16] on

15. Concerning the Orders of Chivalry, let us say that the 'Johannine Church' denotes the totality of all those who were related in any way to what was called in the Middle Ages the 'Kingdom of Prester John', to which we have alluded in our study *The King of the World*.

16. We have seen in a fifteenth-century cemetery capitals in whose sculpture the attributes of love and death are curiously joined.

the other hand, there is also a point of view that establishes an antithesis between love and death, an antithesis that can be explained in part by the very formation of the words [*amour* and *mort*]: the root *mor* is common to both, and, in *a–mor*, is preceded by a privative 'a', as in the Sanskrit *a-mara, a- mrita*, so that 'amour' could be interpreted as a sort of hieroglyphic equivalent for 'immortality'. The 'dead' can in this sense be regarded, in a general way, as designating the profane, whereas the 'living', or those who have attained immortality, are the initiates; and here we should recall the expression 'Land of the Living', synonymous with 'Holy Land' or 'Land of the Saints', 'Pure Land', and so forth; and the opposition that we have just indicated is, in this context, equivalent to the opposition of hell, which is the profane world, to the heavens, which represent the degrees of the initiatic hierarchy.

As for the 'true faith' of which we spoke a while ago, it is designated as the *Fede Santa*, an expression which, like the word *Amore*, applies at the same time to the initiatic organization itself. This *Fede Santa* [Holy Faith], of which Dante was a *Kadosch*, is the faith of the Fedeli d'Amore; and it is also the *Fede dei Santi* [Faith of the Saints]—that is, the *Emounah* of the *Kadosch*, as we explained in *The Esoterism of Dante*. This designation of the initiates as 'Saints', of which *Kadosch* is the Hebrew equivalent, is perfectly understandable if one considers the meaning of the 'heavens' just now indicated, since the heavens are in fact described as the abode of the saints. This must be seen in the context of many other analogous denominations, such as 'Pure Ones', 'Perfect Ones', Cathars, Sufis, Ikhwān-al-Ṣafa' [Brethren of Purity], and so forth, which are all taken in the same sense, permitting us thereby to understand what the 'Holy Land' truly is.[17]

This raises another point to which Valli alludes all too briefly: the secret significance of pilgrimage, which is related to the peregrinations of initiates whose itineraries in fact coincided most frequently with those of ordinary pilgrims, with whom they were thus easily

---

17. It is perhaps not without interest to note further that the initials *F.S.* can also be read as *Fides Sapientia*, an exact translation of the *Pistis Sophia* of the gnostics.

confused, thus permitting them the better to conceal the true reasons for their journeys. Moreover, the very locations of pilgrimage sites such as the sanctuaries of antiquity have an esoteric value that should be taken into consideration here, and this is something directly related to what we have called 'sacred geography'[18] and which must also be considered together with what we have written on the subject of the Compagnons and the Bohemians,[19] a subject to which we shall perhaps return on another occasion.

The question of the 'Holy Land' could also provide the key to the relationship of Dante and the Fedeli d'Amore to the Templars, again a subject that receives very incomplete treatment in Valli's book. Valli does consider these relationships with the Templars, as well as with the alchemists, to be an undeniable fact, and he points out some interesting correspondences, as, for example, that of the Templars' nine-year probation with the symbolic age of nine years in the *Vita Nuova*—but there could have been many other things to choose. Thus, apropos of the Templars' center on Cyprus, it would be interesting to examine the meaning of that island's name, its connection with Venus and the 'third heaven', and the symbolism of copper, from which it took its name, all subjects that we can only point to at the moment, without dwelling on them.

Similarly, regarding the obligation imposed on the Fedeli d'Amore to employ the poetic form in their writings, there would be good reason to ask why poetry was called the 'language of the gods' by the ancients; why *vates* in Latin signified both the poet and the soothsayer or prophet (oracles, moreover, being rendered in verse); why verses were called *carmina* (charms, incantations, a word identical with the Sanskrit *karma*, understood in its technical sense of 'ritual act');[20] and also why it is said of Solomon and other sages, particularly in the Islamic tradition, that they understood the

18. On this subject Grillot de Givry has provided a study entitled 'Les Foyers du mysticisme populaire' in *Voile d'Isis*, April 1920.

19. Cf. *Le Voile d'Isis*, October 1926.

20. *Rita* in Sanskrit signifies what is in conformity with order, a meaning that the adverb *rite* has retained in Latin; the cosmic order is here represented by the law of rhythm.

'language of the birds',[21] which, strange as it may seem, is only another name for the 'language of the gods'.[22]

Before concluding these remarks, we must still say a few words on the interpretation of the *Divine Comedy* that Valli has developed in other works and which he simply summarizes in the work we are now considering. The symmetries of the cross and of the eagle, on which the poem is based entirely, certainly explain a part of its meaning (in conformity, moreover, with the conclusion of *De Monarchia*);[23] but there are in this poem many other things that cannot be completely explained in this way even if we limit ourselves to the use made of symbolic numbers, the author wrongly believing that he has found some single key sufficient to resolve all difficulties. Furthermore, he seems to regard these 'structural connections' as devices peculiar to Dante, whereas, on the contrary, there is something essentially traditional in this symbolic 'architecture', which, although it did not perhaps play a part in the modes of expression customary among the Fedeli d'Amore properly speaking, nonetheless existed in organizations more or less closely allied to their own, and was closely bound to the very art of the builders.[24] There seems to be an intuition of these relationships, however, when he states that 'a study of symbolism in the figurative arts' could further the research in question. Moreover, here, as everywhere, one could discover many other points of comparison, sometimes quite unexpected ones, once all 'aesthetic' preoccupations were laid aside.[25]

If we have dwelt at such length on Valli's book it is because it is one that truly deserves our attention, and if we have especially pointed out its omissions, it is because in this way we are able to indicate for him and for others new paths for research that may successfully complement the results already achieved. It seems that the

21. See 'The Language of the Birds', *Symbols of Sacred Science*, chap. 9.

22. The same thing is also found in the Germanic legends.

23. Cf. *Spiritual Authority and Temporal Power*, chap. 8.

24. We recall the Masonic expression 'fragment of architecture', which applies in the truest sense to the work of Dante.

25. We are thinking especially of certain of the ideas contained in Pierre Piobb's curious book *Le Secret de Nostradamus*, Paris, 1927.

time has come when the true significance of Dante's work may at last be uncovered; if the interpretations of Rossetti and Aroux were not taken seriously in their own times, it is perhaps not because minds were much less prepared to receive them then than they are today, but rather because it was foreseen that the secret must be kept for six centuries (the Chaldean *Naros*). Luigi Valli often speaks of these six centuries during which Dante was not understood, but evidently without seeing any particular meaning in that fact; and this again demonstrates the need, in studies of this kind, for a know-ledge of 'cyclical laws', something the modern West has so completely forgotten.

5

The Secret Language
of Dante AND the
'Fedeli d'Amore' [II]

We devoted the preceding chapter to Luigi Valli's important work of the same title published in 1928; in 1931 we learned of the sudden and premature death of the author, from whom we were hoping for other studies no less worthy of interest; we then received a second volume, bearing the same title as the first and containing responses to objections that had been made to its thesis and some complementary notes.[1]

Nearly all the objections, which attest to an incomprehension that is no cause for surprise, may be subsumed, as was moreover easy to foresee, under one of two headings: those from 'literary critics' well-imbued with scholarly and academic prejudices, and those from Catholic circles, where none want to admit that Dante belonged to an initiatic organization; all concur however, albeit for different reasons, in denying the existence of esoterism, even where it is most strikingly evident. The author seems to attach more importance to the first, which he discusses at far greater length than he does the second; we for our part would be tempted to do just the opposite, seeing in the latter a much graver symptom of the deformation of the modern mentality; but this difference in perspective is to be explained by Valli's chosen point of view, which is exclusively that of a 'researcher' and historian. This all too exterior point of

---

1. *Il linguaggio segreto di Dante e dei Fidèles d'Amour*, vol. II (*Discussione e note aggiunte*); Roma, Biblioteca di Filosofia e Scienza, Casa éditrice 'Optima'.

view gives rise to a certain number of deficiencies and linguistic inaccuracies, which we have had occasion to point out in the previous chapter. Valli acknowledges in connection with just this point that 'he has never had contact with initiatic traditions of any kind,' and that 'his mental training is of a critical nature'; it is all the more remarkable then that he should have arrived at conclusions so far removed from those of ordinary 'criticism', conclusions that are even quite astonishing coming from someone who affirms his wish to be 'a man of the twentieth century'. It is no less regrettable that as a result of prejudice he does not allow himself to understand the notion of traditional orthodoxy; that he persists in applying the disagreeable term 'sect' to organizations of an initiatic, and not religious, character; and that he denies having confused the 'mystical' and the 'initiatic' whereas in fact he does this again throughout this second book. But these shortcomings must not prevent us from recognizing Valli's great merit, 'profane' though he may be and wished to remain, for having glimpsed a great part of the truth despite all the obstacles that his education was naturally bound to put in his way, and for having stated that truth without regard for the opposition he was bound to elicit from all those who have some interest in its remaining unknown.

We shall mention only two or three examples typical of the incomprehension of academic 'critics'. Some have gone so far as to contend that beautiful poetry cannot be symbolic; it seems that for them a work of art cannot be admired unless it has no meaning, and that the existence of a deeper meaning destroys its artistic value! Here we see expressed as clearly as possible that 'profane' conception of art in general and poetry in particular which we have recently had several occasions to describe as a modern degeneration wholly contrary to the character that both arts and sciences possessed originally, and that they have always had in any traditional civilization. Let us note in this regard a rather interesting formulation cited by Valli: in all medieval (as opposed to modern) art, 'what is at stake is the incarnation of an idea, not the idealization of a reality'; we would rather have said 'a reality of a sensible order', for an idea is also a reality, and even one of a superior order, this 'incarnation of an idea' in a particular form being nothing but symbolism itself.

Others have put forward a truly comical objection: they contend that it would be 'vile' to write in 'jargon', that is to say in a language of conventions, evidently regarding this only as a sort of cowardice and dissimulation. To tell the truth, Valli may perhaps have insisted too exclusively, as we have already noted, on the desire of the Fedeli d'Amore to conceal themselves for motives of prudence; it is incontestable that this was indeed the case—it was a necessity imposed on them by circumstances—but this is only the most outward and the least of the reasons justifying their use of a language that was not only conventional but also and above all symbolic. Analogous examples might be found in quite different circumstances, where there would have been no danger in speaking openly, were such a thing possible; and even then one could say that there is an advantage in excluding those not 'qualified', a policy arising from concerns other than simple prudence; but what must be emphasized above all is that truths of a certain order can, by their very nature, only be expressed symbolically.

Finally, there are some who find the existence of symbolic poetry among the Fedeli d'Amore unlikely because it would constitute a 'unique case', whereas Valli was determined to show that the same thing also existed in the East, and at precisely the same time, notably in Persian poetry. One could even add that this symbolism of love has sometimes been used in India as well; and, to confine ourselves to the Islamic world, it is rather singular that one almost always speaks solely of Persian poetry in this regard, whereas similar examples of a no less esoteric nature can readily be found in Arabic poetry, for instance in the work of Omar ibn al-Fārid. And we may add that many other 'veils' were also used in the poetic expressions of Sufism, including that of scepticism, for which one could cite as examples Omar al-Khayyām and Abu'l-Alā al-Ma'arrī. Regarding the latter in particular, there are very few who know that he was an initiate of high rank; and another curious fact of particular relevance to the subject that occupies us at present (and that so far we have not found noted anywhere else) is that his *Risālat al-Ghufrān* could be regarded as one of the principal Islamic 'sources' of the *Divine Comedy.*[2]

As for the obligation imposed upon all members of an initiatic order to write in verse, it is in perfect accord with the character of 'sacred language' which poetry formerly possessed; and as Valli quite justly says, something quite other is involved than merely 'creating literature'. Such was never the aim of Dante and his contemporaries, who, adds Valli ironically, 'were at fault in not having read the books of modern criticism.' Even in very recent times each member of certain Islamic esoteric confraternities was still obliged, on the occasion of the Shaykh's annual *mulid,* to compose a poem in which he would strive, even at the expense of the perfection of form, to incorporate a more or less profound doctrinal meaning.

Regarding Valli's latest remarks, some of which open the way for further research, we shall mention one concerning the relationship of Joachim de Fiore to the Fedeli d'Amore: *Fiore,* taken as a synonym of *Rosa,* is one of the symbols most widely used in the latter's poetry; and under the title of *Fiore* an Italian adaptation of the *Romance of the Rose* was written by a Florentine named Durante, who was almost certainly Dante himself.[3] Moreover, the name of the convent of *San Giovanni in Fiore,* from which *Giocchino di Fiore* took his name, does not appear before his time. Was it he who named it? And if so, why did he choose this name? What is remarkable is that in his writings Joachim de Fiore speaks of a symbolic 'widow', as do also Francesco da Barberino and Boccaccio, both of whom belonged to the Fedeli d'Amore; and we should add that even today this 'widow' is still well-known in Masonic symbolism. In this regard it is regrettable that political preoccupations seem to have prevented Valli from noticing certain striking correspondences; he is undoubtedly right to say that the initiatic organiza-

---

2. Abu'l-Ala al Ma'arri (937–1057), one of the greatest Arab poets, who became blind as a child. Regarding his work *Risālat al-Ghufrān* [Treatise on Pardon], its treatment of the Nocturnal Journey of the Prophet, and its possible role as a precursor to Dante's *Divine Comedy,* see Miguel Asín Palacios, *Islam and the Divine Comedy,* tr. Harold Sutherland (London: Frank Cass & Company, Ltd., 1968), p55. ED.

3. *Dante* is in effect only a contraction of *Durante,* which was his real name.

tions under discussion are not Masonic, but between the Masons and the Fedeli d'Amore the link is no less certain; and is it not curious, for example, that 'wind' in the language of the Fedeli d'Amore should have exactly the same meaning as 'rain' in that of Masonry?

Another important point concerns the relationship between the Fedeli d'Amore and the alchemists. A particularly significant symbol in this regard is found in Francesco da Barberino's *Documenti d'Amore*. The figure in question consists of twelve personages arranged symmetrically and forming six couples which represent as many initiatic degrees, surrounding a single figure at the center; this last, who holds in his hands the symbolic rose, has two heads, one male and one female, and is manifestly identical with the Hermetic *Rebis*. The only notable divergence from the figures that appear in alchemical treatises is that in the latter it is the right side that is masculine and the left feminine, whereas here we find the reverse. This peculiarity seems to have escaped Valli, who nonetheless provides the explanation himself without appearing to be aware of it when he says that 'man with his passive intellect is reunited with the active intelligence, represented by woman,' whereas it is generally the masculine that symbolizes the active element and the feminine the passive. What is most remarkable is that this sort of reversal of the usual relationship is also found in the symbolism of Hindu Tantrism; this parallel compels recognition all the more strongly when we find Cecco d'Ascoli saying 'onde io son ella' [whence I am she], exactly as the *Shaktas*, who instead of *So'ham*, or 'I am He' (the *Ana Huwa* of Islamic esoterism), say *Sa'ham*, or 'I am She'. On the other hand, Valli notes that adjacent to the *Rebis* figure in the *Rosarium Philosophorum* one sees a sort of tree bearing six pairs of faces disposed symmetrically on either side of the trunk, with a single face at the summit which he considers identical with the personages depicted by Francesco da Barberino. It does indeed seem that in both cases an initiatic hierarchy of seven degrees is involved, the last degree being characterized essentially as the reconstitution of the Hermetic androgyne, that is to say, in short, the restoration of the 'primordial state'. And this in turn accords with what we have had occasion to say about the significance of the term 'Rose-Cross' as designating the perfection of the human state. As regards the seven degrees of initiation, we have alluded to the ladder of seven rungs in our study *The Esoterism of Dante*. It is true that these rungs are generally related to the seven planetary heavens, which refer to supra-human states, but by reason of analogy there must be a hierarchical correspondence in an initiatic system between the 'lesser' and the 'greater' mysteries. Then again, the being reintegrated into the center of the human state is by this very fact ready to rise to the superior states and already dominates the conditions of existence in this world of which it has become master; that is why the *Rebis* of the *Rosarium Philosophorum* has the moon beneath its feet, and that of Basil Valentine a dragon. This significance was completely misunderstood by Valli, who saw therein only symbols of corrupted doctrine or 'the error that oppresses the world,' whereas in reality the moon represents the domain of forms—this symbolism being the same as that of 'walking on the waters'—and the dragon, in this context the elemental world.

Harboring no doubts about Dante's links with the Templars, of which many indications exist, Valli also raises the subject of the medallion in the Vienna Museum which we mentioned in *The Esoterism of Dante*. When he went to inspect this medallion he discovered that its two sides had been joined together at a late date, suggesting that it must have been put together originally from two separate medallions; moreover, he recognized that this singular operation could not have been performed without some reason. As for the initials F. S. K. I. P. F. T., which figure on the medallion's reverse side, for him they represent the initials of the seven virtues, *Fides, Spes, Karitas, Justitia, Prudentia, Fortitudo, Temperantia*, despite their anomalous arrangement in two rows of four and three, rather than of three and four, as the distinction between the three theological virtues and the four cardinal virtues would require. Joined as they are to laurel and olive branches, 'which are the two sacred plants of initiates,' he admits that his interpretation does not necessarily exclude the existence of another, more hidden, significance; and we might add that the abnormal spelling *Karitas* rather than *Charitas* could well have been necessitated precisely by this double meaning. Elsewhere in the same study we pointed out the initiatic role attributed to the three theological virtues, still preserved in the

eighteenth degree of Scottish Freemasonry;[4] furthermore, the septenary of the virtues is composed of a higher ternary and a lower
quaternary, which sufficiently indicates that it is constituted according to esoteric principles; and finally, this septenary, quite as well as
that of the 'liberal arts', also divided into *trivium* and *quadrivium*,
corresponds to the seven rungs to which we alluded earlier, all the
more so as 'faith' (the *Fede Santa*) is in fact always represented on
the highest rung of the 'mysterious ladder' of the *Kadosch*. All this
therefore constitutes a far more coherent whole than superficial
observers may believe.

While at the Vienna Museum Valli also discovered Dante's original medallion, the reverse side of which represents a still more
strange and enigmatic figure: a heart placed at the center of a system
of circles that has the appearance of (though it is not in fact) a celestial sphere, and which is not accompanied by any inscription.[5]
There are three meridional circles and four latitudinal circles, which
Valli again relates respectively to the three theological and the four
cardinal virtues. What leads us to regard this interpretation as correct is above all the accurate application made in this arrangement
of the vertical and the horizontal directions to the relationships of
the contemplative and the active life, or to the respective jurisdic-
tions of the spiritual authority and the temporal power, to which
the two groups of virtues correspond. An oblique circle, completing
the figure (and forming with the others the number eight—that of
equilibrium), links everything in a perfect harmony under the irra-
diation of the 'doctrine of love'.[6]

A final point concerns the secret name that was given God by
the Fedeli d'Amore: in his *Tractatus Amoris* Francesco da Barberino

---

4. In the seventeenth grade, that of 'Knight of the East and West', one also finds
a device formed of seven initials, those of a septenary of divine attributes whose
enumeration is drawn from a passage in the Apocalypse.

5. This heart so placed reminds us of the no less remarkable and mysterious
figure of the heart of Saint-Denis d'Orques, shown in the center of the planetary
and zodiacal circles, a figure that was the subject of a study by Charbonneau-Lassay
in *Regnabit*.

6. On this subject, the reader is referred to what we have said about Dante's
treatise *De Monarchia* in our *Spiritual Authority and Temporal Power*.

represented himself in an attitude of adoration before the letter 'I';
and in the *Divine Comedy* Adam says that the first name of God was
'I',[7] the one that came afterward being *El*. This letter 'I', which Dante
calls the 'ninth figure' in accordance with its place in the Latin
alphabet (and we know what symbolic importance the number
nine[8] held for him), is evidently no other than the *yod*, although this
is the tenth letter of the Hebrew alphabet; and in fact, apart from
being the first letter of the tetragrammaton, the *yod* is itself a divine
name, whether in isolation or repeated three times.[9] It is this same
yod that in Masonry became the letter 'G' by assimilation with 'God'
(for it was in England that this transformation took place), this
without prejudice to the many other secondary meanings that came
to be centered in this same letter 'G', but which it is not our intention to examine here.

Saddened as we are by Valli's passing, we hope all the more that
he will have successors in his chosen field of research, which is as
vast as it is yet unexplored. It does seem that this will be the case, for
he himself informs us that he has already been followed by Gaetano
Scarlata, who has devoted a work[10] to the special study of Dante's
treatise *De vulgari eloquentia*. The book in question is also 'full of
mysteries', as Rossetti and Aroux so well perceived, and though it
seems to treat simply of the Italian language it relates in fact to a
secret language. This procedure is also customary in Islamic esoterism, where, as we have pointed out on another occasion, an initiatic
work may assume the appearance of a simple treatise on grammar.
Many more discoveries no doubt remain to be made in the same
order of ideas, and even if those who devote themselves to this
research bring to it personally only a 'profane' mentality (provided

7. *Paradiso*, xxvi, 133.

8. The French text here gives the Arabic numeral 4, which is quite likely a mis-
print as the number four is not under consideration. Ed.

9. Is it merely coincidental that the heart of Saint-Denis d'Orques, which we
just mentioned, bears what appears to be a wound in the form of *yod*? Would there
not be some reason to suppose that the depictions of the 'Sacred Heart' antedating
its 'official' adoption by the Church may have had certain links with the doctrine of
the Fedeli d'Amore or of their successors?

10. *Le origini della letteratura italiana nel pensiero di Dante*, Palermo, 1930.

however that it be unbiased) and see in it only the object of a sort of historical curiosity, the results obtained will be no less able, both in themselves and for those who know how to understand their true and full significance, to contribute effectively to a restoration of the traditional spirit. Do not these labors relate, however unconsciously or involuntarily, to the 'search for the Lost Word', which is the same as the 'quest for the Holy Grail'?

6

New Insights
Into the Secret
Language of Dante

When speaking previously of the two editions of Luigi Valli's last book, we mentioned a work along similar lines by Gaetano Scarlata devoted to Dante's treatise *De vulgari eloquentia*, or rather, as Scarlata prefers to call it (for the title has never been exactly fixed), *De vulgaris eloquentiae doctrina*, following the expression Dante himself employed at the outset when defining its subject matter in order to make evident his intentions as to the doctrinal content of poetry in the common [*vulgar*] tongue.[1] Indeed, those whom Dante calls *poeti vulgari* are those whose writings had, as he says, *verace intendimento*, that is, contained a hidden meaning in conformity with the symbolism of the Fedeli d'Amore, since he opposes them to the *litterali* (not the incorrect *litterati*, as one sometimes reads) or those who wrote with only a literal meaning. For Dante, the first are true poets, whom he also calls *trilingues doctores*, which can be understood in an outward sense since such poetry existed in Italian, Provençal (not 'French', as Scarlata incorrectly states) and Spanish; but in reality, since no poet ever actually wrote in all three languages, the term signifies that the poetry should be interpreted according to a threefold meaning; and on the subject of these *trilingues doctores*, Dante says *maxime conveniunt in hoc vocabulo quod*

---

1. *Le origini della letteratura italiana nel pensiero di Dante*, Palermo, 1930.

est Amor [they most agree in that name which is Love], which is a rather obvious allusion to the doctrine of the Fedeli d'Amore.[2]

On the subject of these latter, Scarlata makes the very appropriate observation that they must never have constituted an association following rigorously defined forms, more or less similar to those of modern Masonry for example, with a central authority establishing 'branches' in various localities; and we might add in support of this view that in Masonry itself no such organization existed until the Grand Lodge was established in England in 1717. Moreover, it does not seem that Scarlata has grasped the full import of this fact, which he believes must be attributed simply to circumstances unfavorable to the stable outward existence of such an institution. In reality, as we have already often said, a truly initiatic organization cannot be a 'society' in the modern sense of the word, with all the external formalism that this implies: when statutes, written rules, and other things of that nature appear, it is certain that some degeneration is present, imparting to the organization a 'semi-profane' character, if one may use such an expression. But as concerns what belongs to a properly initiatic order, Scarlata has not gone to the heart of the matter and seems not even to have gotten as far as Valli. He sees above all the political aspect, which is on the whole accessory, and speaks constantly of 'sects', a point upon which we explained ourselves amply in the preceding chapter. In his treatment of the subject he draws but few consequences from the affirmation of the doctrine (esoteric, not heretical) of the *amor sapientiae*, which, however, is absolutely essential, the rest depending solely on historical contingencies. It is possible, moreover, that the subject of this study has lent itself quite readily to what appears to us an error of perspective: the *De vulgaris eloquentiae doctrina* has a direct link to the *De Monarchia,* and is consequently associated with that part of Dante's work where social applications occupy the most important place. But can these applications themselves be properly under-

---

2. One must undoubtedly understand by this three meanings superior to the literal one, so that all together one would have the four meanings Dante speaks of in the *Convito,* as we indicated at the beginning of our study *The Esoterism of Dante.*

stood if one does not constantly refer them to their principle? What is most regrettable is that when he turns to general historical considerations Scarlata permits himself to be drawn into interpretations that are more than questionable: does he not go so far as to portray Dante and the Fedeli d'Amore as adversaries of the spirit of the Middle Ages and precursors of modern ideas, animated by a 'secular' and 'democratic' spirit that would in reality be the most 'anti-initiatic' thing conceivable? This second part of his book, although it contains some interesting bits of information, particularly on the Eastern influences at the court of Frederick II and in the Franciscan movement, would be worth taking up on a basis more in conformity with traditional interpretations. It is true, however, that the book is only presented as a 'first attempt at historical reconstruction,' and who knows but that the author may not be led by his subsequent research to rectify it himself?

One cause of Scarlata's misunderstanding is perhaps to be found in the way Dante contrasts the use of the *vulgare* [vernacular] to that of Latin, an ecclesiastical language, and also in the way poets use symbols, according to the *verace intendimento*, which he contrasts with that of the theologians (their way being rather that of simple allegory); but it was in the eyes of Dante's adversaries or (which often amounts to the same thing) of those who did not understand him that the *vulgare* could be no more than the *sermo laicus*, whereas for himself it was something altogether different; and furthermore, from the strictly traditional point of view, is not the function of initiates more truly 'sacerdotal' than that of an exoteric 'clergy' that knows only the letter and adheres to the shell of the doctrine?[3] The essential point here is to ascertain what Dante means by the expression *vulgare illustre*, an expression that may seem strange and even contradictory if one holds to the ordinary sense of the words, but which becomes self-evident when one understands that for him *vulgare* is synonymous with *naturale*. It is the language that man learns directly through oral transmission (just as the child, who from the initiatic point of view represents the

---

3. According to the normal hierarchical order, the initiate is above the 'clergy' (even if the latter are theologians), while the 'laity' is naturally below the latter.

neophyte, learns its own mother tongue), that is, symbolically speaking, the language that serves as the vehicle for the tradition, and that may in this respect be identified with the primordial and universal language, a point touching closely on the question of the mysterious 'Syriac language' (*lughat suryaniyyah*) of which we have spoken in previous articles;[4] and while it is true that for Dante this 'language of revelation' seems to have been Hebrew, such an affirmation, as we were just saying, should not be taken literally, for the same thing might be said of any language that has a 'sacred' character, that is to say which serves to express a regular traditional form.[5] According to Dante, the language spoken by the first man and directly created by God was perpetuated by his descendants down to the raising of the Tower of Babel; afterward, *hanc formam locutionis hereditati sunt filii Heber...* ; *hiis solis post confusionem remansit* ['this form of speech was inherited by the sons of Heber...; to them alone did it remain after the confusion (of tongues)']; but these 'sons of Heber', are they not all those who have kept the tradition rather than any specific people? Has not the name 'Israel' often been employed to designate the totality of initiates, whatever their ethnic origin, who in fact really constitute the 'chosen people', and who possess the universal language that enables them all to understand each other, that is, the knowledge of the one tradition that is concealed beneath all its particular forms?[6] Moreover, if Dante had really thought it was the Hebrew language that was in question, he would not have been able to say that the Church (designated by the enigmatic name *Petramala*) believes it speaks the language of Adam, for the Church speaks not Hebrew but Latin, for which no one yet, it seems, has claimed the quality of a primeval language; but if one understands Dante's phrase to mean that the Church

4. 'The Science of Letters (*'Ilm al-ḥurūf)*', *Symbols of Sacred Science*, chap. 8, and 'The Language of the Birds', ibid., chap. 9.

5. It goes without saying that when we oppose 'vulgar languages' to 'sacred languages', we take the word 'vulgar' in its usual sense; if we took it in Dante's sense, this expression would no longer apply, and we ought rather to say 'profane languages' to avoid all ambiguity.

6. See on this subject the study 'The Gift of Tongues' in *Perspectives on Initiation*, chap. 37.

believes it teaches the true doctrine of revelation, everything becomes perfectly intelligible. What is more, even if we admit that the early Christians, who possessed this true doctrine, actually spoke Hebrew (which would be historically inexact, for Aramaic is no more Hebrew than Italian is Latin), the Fedeli d'Amore, who considered themselves their successors, never pretended to reclaim this language in order to oppose it to Latin, as they should logically have had to do if it were necessary to keep to the literal interpretation.[7]

We see then that what is at issue is far removed from the purely 'philological' significance usually attributed to Dante's treatise, and that something quite other than the Italian language is involved; and even what genuinely relates to the latter may also have, at the same time, a symbolic value. Thus, when Dante opposes such and such a city or region to another, it is never simply a question of linguistic opposition; and when he cites certain names, such as *Petramala, Papienses*, or *Aquilegienses*, there are in these choices (even without going so far as to consider geographical symbolism strictly speaking) fairly transparent intentions, as Rossetti had already noted; and naturally, in order to understand the real meaning of many apparently insignificant words, it is often necessary to refer back to the conventional terminology of the Fedeli d'Amore. Scarlata quite rightly points out that it is almost always the examples (including those that appear to have only a purely rhetorical or grammatical value) that furnish the key to the context; this was indeed an excellent means of diverting the attention of the 'profane', who could have seen in them only some commonplace phrases of no importance. It might be said that these examples play a role comparable to that of the 'myths' in the Platonic dialogues, and one need only look at what the academic critics make of these to entertain no further doubts as to the perfect efficacy of the strategy that

7. We would also add that, as Scarlata notes, the idea of the continuation of the primordial language is contradicted by the words Dante himself attributes to Adam in the *Divine Comedy* (*Paradiso*, xxvi, 124), words that may be explained moreover through consideration of the cyclical periods: the original language was *tutta spenta* [totally spent] after the *Krita-Yuga* ended, and hence well before the enterprise of the 'people of Nimrod', which corresponds only to the beginning of the *Kali-Yuga*.

consists in offering as an *hors d'oeuvre*, so to speak, what is precisely the main course.

In short, what Dante seems to have had in mind was essentially the establishment of a language capable, by virtue of a superimposition of multiple meanings, of expressing as far as possible the esoteric doctrine; and if the codification of such a language can be qualified as 'rhetoric', it is in any case a very special kind of rhetoric, as far removed from what is understood by that word today as is the poetry of the Fedeli d'Amore from that of the moderns, whose predecessors are those 'litterali' whom Dante reproached for versifying 'foolishly' (*stoltamente*) and failing to put into their lines any profound meaning.[8] According to Valli's expression, which we have already quoted, Dante set himself quite a different task from 'creating literature', which amounts to saying that he was precisely the complete opposite of a modern author; his work, far from being contrary to the spirit of the Middle Ages, is one of its most perfect syntheses, in the same rank as that of the cathedral builders; and the simplest initiatic facts enable us to understand without difficulty that there are very profound reasons for this correspondence.

---

8. In more or less the same way the predecessors of the present-day chemists were, not the true alchemists, but the 'puffers'; whether in the sciences or in the arts, the purely 'profane' conceptions of the moderns always result in a similar degeneration.

7

'Fedeli d'Amore'
and 'Courts of Love'

Research in Italy on the Fedeli d'Amore continues to give rise to interesting works. Alfonso Ricolfi, already known for some articles on this subject, has just published a study, to be followed by others, in which he states his intention to take up the work left unfinished by Luigi Valli.[1] Perhaps he does so with some reservations, however, for he considers that Valli has 'exaggerated' certain points, particularly in denying, contrary to the most common opinion, the real existence of all the women extolled by the poets attached to the Fedeli d'Amore. But in truth this question is no doubt less important than he seems to think, at least if one places oneself outside the point of view of simple historical curiosity, and it has no bearing whatsoever on a true interpretation of the work. Indeed, there is nothing impossible about the idea that in designating the divine Wisdom by a feminine name certain poets may in a purely symbolic way have adopted the name of a woman who had actually lived, and there are at least two reasons for doing so: firstly, as we had occasion to say recently, anything at all can, according to the nature of the individual, provide the occasion and starting-point for a spiritual development, and this may be true of an earthly love as well as of any other circumstance (all the more so as what we are dealing with here, lest we forget, can be characterized as a path for the Kshatriyas); and secondly, the real meaning of the name so used became the

1. *Studi sui fidele d'amore I. Le Corti d'Amore ed i loro riflessi in Italia*; Roma, Biblioteca della *Nuove Rivista Storica*, Societa Editrice Dante Alighieri, 1933.

more impenetrable to the profane, who naturally held to the literal meaning, and this advantage, although of a contingent order, was perhaps not entirely negligible.

This remark leads us to consider another point closely related to the preceding. Ricolfi deems it necessary to distinguish between 'Courts of Love' and 'courts of love'; and this distinction is not the mere subtlety it may seem at first glance. Indeed, one must understand by 'Court of Love' a symbolic assemblage presided over by Love itself personified, whereas a 'court of love' is only a human gathering, a sort of tribunal called upon to adjudicate more or less complex cases. Whether these cases were real or imaginary, or, in other words, whether they involved effective jurisdiction or simply a game (and they may in fact have been both), matters very little from our point of view. If they were truly only occupied with questions of profane love, the 'courts of love' were not assemblies of the genuine Fedeli d'Amore (unless they sometimes assumed this aspect outwardly in order to better disguise themselves); but they may have been an imitation and a kind of parody born of the incomprehension of the uninitiated, just as during the same period there were undoubtedly profane poets who celebrated real women in their verse and put nothing more in their poetry than a literal meaning. Likewise there were 'puffers' alongside the true alchemists, and here too we must beware of any confusion between the two groups, something not always easy to do without a thorough examination, for outwardly their language may be identical; and this same confusion may in fact have sometimes served, in both cases, to turn aside injudicious prying.

However, it is not admissible to attribute any sort of precedence or priority to what is counterfeit or degenerate; and Ricolfi seems disposed to allow too readily that the deeper meaning may have been added after the fact to something that at first would have had only an altogether profane character. With regard to this point we will be content to recall, as we have often done, that all art and science has an initiatic origin and that their strictly traditional character can have been lost only as a result of the incomprehension we have just mentioned; to assume the reverse is to admit an influence of the profane world upon the initiatic world, that is to say a reversal of the true hierarchical relationships inherent in the very nature of things. What might give rise to such an illusion in the present case is that the profane imitation must always have been more visible than the true Fedeli d'Amore, who, moreover, were an organization that should not be considered a 'society', as we have already explained with regard to initiatic organizations in general.[2] If the Fedeli d'Amore seems to evade the ordinary historian, this is proof not of its non-existence, but, on the contrary, of its truly serious and profound character.[3]

One of the principal merits of Ricolfi's work is that it discloses new evidence for the existence of the Fedeli d'Amore in Northern France; and the little-known poem by Jacques de Baisieux on the *Fiefs d'Amour* (identified with the 'celestial estates' [*fiefs célestes*] in contrast to the 'terrestrial estates' [*fiefs terrestres*]), about which he speaks at length, is particularly significant in this respect. The traces of such an organization are certainly much rarer in that region than in the Languedoc and Provence,[4] but we must not forget that a short time later the *Romance of the Rose* appeared; and, in another connection, close links with the 'Knighthood of the Grail' (to which Jacques de Baisieux himself explicitly alludes) are suggested by the fact that Chrétien de Troyes translated the *Ars Amandi* [The Art of Love] of Ovid, which also may well have some other meaning beside its literal one, something that should occasion no surprise given that Ovid is also the author of the *Metamorphoses*. Nor by any means has everything been said on the subject of 'knight-errantry', the very conception of which is connected with that of initiatic 'journeys';

---

2. Cf. *Perspectives on Initiation*.

3. Let us recall further a propos of this that it can in no way be a matter of a 'sect': the initiatic domain is not the domain of exoteric religion, and the formation of religious 'sects' can only have been another instance of profane degeneration. We regret finding again in Ricolfi's work a certain confusion between the two domains, which greatly impedes an understanding of what is really involved.

4. Is it merely a coincidence that in the Compagnonnage the 'Tour de France' leaves aside the whole of the northern region, and includes mostly towns situated south of the Loire, or should we not see herein something the origin of which may go much further back and of which the underlying reasons, it goes without saying, are nowadays entirely lost from view?

but for the moment we must restrict ourselves to recalling what we have already written on this last subject, adding only that the expression 'wild knights' [*chevaliers sauvages*], which Ricolfi mentions, would merit a separate study.

Some rather strange things are also to be found in the book of André, chaplain of the King of France; unfortunately this for the most part escaped Ricolfi's attention and he only reports a few of them, without seeing therein anything extraordinary. For instance, it is said in this book that the palace of Love rises 'in the center of the Universe,' and that it has four sides and four gateways; the east gateway is reserved for the god, and the north remains forever closed. Now here is something remarkable: according to Masonic traditions the Temple of Solomon, which symbolizes the 'Center of the World', also takes the form of a quadrilateral or 'long square' with gateways opening on three of its sides, the north side alone having no opening; if there is a slight difference (absence of a gateway in the one case, gateway closed in the other), the symbolism is nevertheless exactly the same since the north is here the dark side, which the light of the sun does not reach.[5] Moreover, Love appears here in the form of a king bearing on his head a crown of gold; and is this not how we also see him represented in Scottish Freemasonry at the grade of 'Prince of Mercy',[6] and might we not say that he is therefore the 'king of peace', which is the very meaning of Solomon's name? And there is yet another parallel which is no less striking: in various poems and fables, the 'Court of Love' is described as composed entirely of birds who take turns speaking; now we have previously explained what is to be understood by the 'language of the birds',[7] and would it be reasonable to see nothing but a coincidence in the

5. This is the *yin* aspect of the Chinese tradition, the opposite aspect being that of *yang*; and this observation might help resolve the controversial question of the respective positions of the two symbolic columns: the one to the North must normally correspond to the feminine principle; that to the South, to the masculine.

6. See *The Esoterism of Dante.* In one of his articles for the *Corriere Padano* Ricolfi has himself studied the particular meaning given by the Fedeli d'Amore to the word *Merzé*, which clearly seems to have been one of the enigmatic names for their organization.

7. See our study on this subject in *Symbols of Sacred Science*, chap. 9.

fact that, as we have already pointed out, it is precisely in connection with Solomon that this 'language of the birds' is explicitly mentioned in the Koran? Let us add yet another point that is also not without interest in establishing other concordances: the principal roles in this 'Court of Love' generally seem to be attributed to the nightingale and the parrot. The importance accorded the nightingale in Persian poetry is well-known, and the interconnection with the poetry of the Fedeli d'Amore has already been pointed out by Luigi Valli; but what is perhaps less well-known is that the parrot is the *vāhana*, or symbolic vehicle of *Kāma*, that is, the Hindu *Eros*. Is there not much for further reflection here? And while we are on the subject of birds, is it not also curious that in his *Documenti d'Amore* Francesco da Barberino represents Love itself with the feet of a falcon or a sparrow-hawk, the bird emblematic of the Egyptian *Horus*, of which the symbolism has a close connection with that of the 'Heart of the World'?[8]

Speaking of Francesco da Barberino, Ricolfi returns to the figure already mentioned[9] in which six couples symmetrically arranged, and a thirteenth, androgynous, figure at the center, quite clearly represent seven initiatic degrees. If his interpretation differs somewhat from Valli's, it is only on points of detail that do not at all alter its essential significance. He also reproduces a second figure, a representation of a 'Court of Love' where the characters are arranged on eleven tiers. This last fact does not seem to have attracted Ricolfi's attention particularly, but if one recalls what we have said elsewhere on the role of this number eleven for Dante in connection with the symbolism of certain initiatic organizations,[10] its importance should easily be understood. It seems, moreover, that the author of the *Documenti d'Amore* may even have been acquainted with a certain specialized kind of traditional knowledge, such as the

8. Charbonneau-Lassay has devoted a study to this subject in the review *Regnabit*.

9. See chapter 5 above.

10. *The Esoterism of Dante*, chap. 7. Ricolfi seems moreover quite disposed to accept the links between the Fedeli d'Amore and the Templars, although he only alludes to them in passing, this question standing outside the subject he proposed to treat.

explication of the meaning of words through the elucidation of their constituent elements. Indeed, read attentively the following phrase in which he defines one of the twelve virtues corresponding to the twelve parts of his work (this number also has its raison d'être: a zodiac wherein Love is the sun), but which Ricolfi quotes without comment: *Docilitas, data novitiis notitia vitiorum, docet illos ab illorum vilitate abstinere.*[11] Is there not something here that recalls, for example, Plato's *Cratylus?*[12]

Before leaving the subject of Francesco da Barberino, let us further point out a rather curious mistake Ricolfi has made with regard to his androgynous emblem, which is clearly Hermetic and has absolutely nothing to do with 'magic', these being altogether different things. He even goes so far as to speak in this connection of 'white magic', whereas he is inclined to see 'black magic' in the *Rebis* of Basil Valentine because of the dragon which, as we have already said,[13] merely represents the elemental world (and which, moreover, is placed beneath the feet of the *Rebis* and is thus dominated by it), and, even more amusingly, also because of the set-square and the compass, for reasons that are only too easy to guess and undoubtedly depend more on political contingencies than on considerations of an initiatic order! And finally, to end, since Ricolfi seems to be in some doubt as to the esoteric character of the figure where, under the form of a simple 'illuminated letter', Francesco da Barberino had

11. This phrase translates as 'Docility, when it has given the novices knowledge of their vices, will teach them to refrain from their baseness,' but Guénon's point rather revolves around the Latin roots that recur in several key words, a point which he does not further develop here. ED.

12. In a more recent era we find a similar procedure employed in a much more obvious way in an Hermetic treatise by Cesare della Riviera entitled *Il Mondo magico degli Heroi* (see our account in *Le Voile d'Isis*, Oct. 1932). Similarly, when Jacques de Baisieux says that *a-mor* signifies 'deathless', one must not hasten to declare, as does Ricolfi, that this is 'false etymology'; for in reality etymology is not in question here, but rather a method of interpretation comparable to the *nirukta* of the Hindu tradition; and without knowing anything of the poem in question, we had pointed to this explanation ourselves, adding to it a comparison with the Sanskrit words *a-mara* and *a-mrita* in our first article devoted to the works of Luigi Valli, which became chapter 4 of this book.

13. See chapter 5 above.

himself represented in adoration before the letter 'I', let us clarify further the significance of this letter. According to Dante, this was the primordial name of God, designating properly the 'Divine Unity' (which, moreover, is why this name is primordial, since the unity of essence necessarily precedes the multiplicity of attributes). Indeed, not only is it the equivalent of the Hebrew *yod*, hieroglyph of the Principle and itself principle of all the other letters of the alphabet, and of which its numerical value of ten reduces to unity (namely the unity displayed in the quaternary: $1 + 2 + 3 + 4 = 10$, or that of the central point that through its expansion produces the circle of universal manifestation); not only does the letter 'I' itself represent unity in Latin numeration by reason of its lineal form, which is the simplest of all geometric forms (a point being strictly speaking 'formless'); but, further still, in the Chinese language the word *i* signifies 'unity' and *Taï-i* is the 'Great Unity', symbolically represented as residing in the pole star, which is again full of meaning, for, coming back to the letter 'I' in Western alphabets, we notice that, being vertical, it is for that very reason apt to symbolize the 'World Axis', of which the importance in all traditional doctrines is quite well known;[14] and thus this 'primordial name of God' recalls to us also the anteriority of 'polar' symbolism in relation to 'solar' symbolism.

We have called attention here mainly to the points where Ricolfi's explanations are patently unsatisfactory, for we think this most useful in the present context; but it goes without saying that it would be unfair to hold against specialists in 'literary historicism', whose training has not touched on the esoteric domain, their lack of the data required to discern and correctly interpret initiatic symbols. On the contrary, we should recognize their merit in daring to go against the grain of officially accepted opinions and anti-traditional interpretations that are imposed by the profane spirit dominating the modern world, and we should thank them for putting at our

14. In operative Masonry the plumb-line, a figure for the 'World Axis', is suspended from the pole star or from the letter 'G', which in this case takes its place and is itself, as we have already pointed out, only a substitute for the Hebraic *yod* (cf. *The Great Triad*, chap. 25).

disposal, by impartially disclosing the results of their research, documents wherein we may discover what they themselves did not see; and we can only hope that more works of this kind will soon be forthcoming and will shed new light on the exceedingly mysterious and complex subject of the initiatic organizations in the Western Middle Ages.

8

The Holy Grail

Arthur Edward Waite has published a work on the legends of the Holy Grail[1] that is imposing in its size and in its extent of research. Anyone interested in the subject of the Grail will find herein a very complete and methodical exposition of the contents of the many texts it mentions, as well as diverse theories that have been proposed to explain the origins and significance of these legends, which are complex and at times even contradictory in certain of their elements. It must be added that Waite's intention was not merely to publish a work of erudition, and for this too he should be commended; we are entirely in agreement with him on the minimal value of all labors that do not exceed this point of view and of which the interest, in short, can only be 'documentary'. His aim was to bring out the real and 'inner' significance of the symbolism of the Holy Grail and of the 'quest'. We are obliged to say, however, that this aspect of his work is unfortunately the one that seems least satisfactory and that the conclusions he arrives at are even rather disappointing, all the more so when one thinks of all the work expended to reach them; and it is on this aspect that we should like to formulate some observations that will, quite naturally, relate to questions we have already treated on other occasions.

We do not believe we do Waite an injustice to say that his work is somewhat *one-sighted*;[2] in French one might say 'partial', though this would not be strictly exact, and in any case we do not mean to

---

1. *The Holy Grail: The Galahad Quest in the Arthurian Literature* [most recent edition: New Hyde Park, NY: University Books, 1961)].
2. The French text has 'one-sighted' italicized and in English. ED.

70

suggest that he intended that it be so. Rather, it has more to do with that failing so common among those who have 'specialized' in a particular order of studies to incline toward reducing everything to it and to neglect whatever cannot be made to fit it. That the legend is Christian is incontestable, and Waite is right to say so; but does that necessarily preclude its being something else at the same time? Those who are conscious of the fundamental unity of all traditions will see no incompatibility here, but for his part, Waite is unwilling to see anything but what is specifically Christian, confining himself to a particular traditional form of which the connection with other forms, precisely through its 'inner' aspect, seems thereby to escape him. Not that he denies the existence of elements from another source, probably anterior to Christianity, for this would go against the evidence; but he accords these only a minor importance and seems to consider them somehow 'accidental', as though they had become attached to the legend 'from outside' simply in consequence of the environment in which it was elaborated. Hence he views these elements as deriving from what is commonly called 'folklore', not always to belittle them, as the name itself might suggest, but more to satisfy a certain contemporary 'fashion' and not always taking account of the intentions implied therein, and on which it may be of some interest to dwell a bit further.

The very concept of 'folklore' as it is commonly understood rests on the radically false idea that there exist 'popular creations', spontaneous products of the masses; and one can immediately see the close relationship between this way of looking at things and 'democratic' prejudices. As has been quite rightly said, 'the profound interest of all so-called popular traditions lies above all in the fact that they are not popular in origin';[3] and we would add that if, as is almost always the case, we are dealing with elements that are traditional in the true sense of the word, however deformed, diminished, or fragmentary they may sometimes be, and with things of real symbolic value, then their origin, far from being popular, is not

---

3. Luc Benoist, *La Cuisine des Anges, une esthétique de la pensée* (Paris: Pelleton, 1932), p 74.

even human. What may be popular is uniquely the fact of 'survival' when these elements come from traditional forms that have disappeared; and in this respect the term 'folklore' takes on a meaning very near to that of 'paganism', taking the latter in its etymological sense and with no polemical or abusive intent. The people thus preserve, without understanding them, the debris of ancient traditions sometimes even reaching back to a past too remote to be determined and which is therefore consigned to the obscure domain of 'prehistory'; and in so doing they function as a more or less 'subconscious' collective memory, of which the content has manifestly come from somewhere else.[4] What may seem most astonishing is that, when we go to the root of the matter, the things so conserved are found to contain in a more or less veiled form a considerable body of esoteric data, that is, what is least 'popular' in essence, and this fact of itself suggests an explanation that we will lay out in a few words. When a traditional form is on the verge of extinction, its last representatives may very well deliberately entrust to this collective memory of which we have just spoken what would otherwise be irrevocably lost. This, in short, is the only way to save what can, at least in some measure, be saved; and, at the same time, the natural incomprehension of the masses is a sufficient guarantee that whatever possesses an esoteric character will not be despoiled in the process but will remain as a sort of witness to the past for those in later times who may be capable of understanding it.

Having said this, we see no reason without closer examination to attribute to 'folklore' everything that pertains to traditions other than Christianity, as though the latter alone were an exception; such seems to be Waite's intention however when he accepts this attribution for all the 'pre-Christian'—and especially the Celtic—elements in the Grail legends. From the perspective of the explanation just given there is no traditional form that is privileged; the only distinction to be made is between forms that have disappeared and those still living. The issue then comes down to knowing

---

4. This is an essentially 'lunar' function, and it should be noted that, astrologically, the popular masses effectively correspond to the moon, which at the same time indicates their purely passive nature, incapable of initiative or spontaneity.

whether or not the Celtic tradition was really no longer living when the legends in question were being elaborated, and this is at least debatable: on the one hand, this tradition may have endured longer than is com-monly believed, with a more or less hidden organization; on the other, the legends themselves may be far older than the 'critics' imagine; not that there need have been texts now lost (we do not believe this any more than Waite does), but there may have been an oral transmission that lasted several centuries, which would not be at all exceptional. For our part, we see here the sign of a 'conjuncture' between two traditional forms, one ancient and the other then still new, the Celtic and the Christian, a conjuncture through which what was to be conserved of the first was, as it were, incorporated into the second, no doubt being modified in its out-ward form to some extent by adaptation and assimilation, but not by transposition to another plane as Waite would have it, for there are equivalences between all regular traditions. The issue therefore is quite other than a simple question of 'sources' as understood by the erudite. It would perhaps be difficult to specify exactly when and where this conjuncture occurred, but this has only a secondary and primarily historical interest; it is, moreover, easy to imagine that such events are unlikely to leave traces in written 'documents'. Perhaps the 'Celtic' or 'Culdean' church merits more attention in this regard than Waite seems disposed to grant it; its very name might lead one to think so, and there is nothing improbable in the suggestion that behind this church there may have been something of a different order, no longer religious, but initiatic, for, like all that pertains to links between different traditions, what is here in question necessarily derives from the initiatic or esoteric domain. Exoterism, whether religious or not, never goes beyond the limits of the traditional form to which it properly belongs; whatever goes beyond these limits cannot belong to a 'church' as such, which can only be its external 'support', a point we shall have occasion to return to later.

Another observation concerning symbolism more particularly here imposes itself: there are symbols that are common to the most diverse and widespread traditional forms, not as a result of 'borrowings', which would in many cases be quite impossible, but because they really belong to the primordial tradition whence, directly or indirectly, all these forms have issued. This is precisely the case with the vase or cup. Why should what relates thereto be merely 'folklore' when present in 'pre-Christian' traditions, whereas in Christianity alone it is an essentially 'eucharistic' symbol? The assimilations envisaged by Bournouf[5] and others like him are not to be rejected here, but rather the 'naturalistic' interpretations some have wished to impose on Christianity as on everything else, interpretations that are in fact nowhere valid. What needs to be done, then, runs exactly contrary to the procedure of Waite, who, confining himself to external and superficial explanations, which he takes on faith so long as they do not concern Christianity, sees radically different and unrelated meanings where there are only more or less multiple aspects of the same symbol or of its various applications. It would no doubt have been otherwise had he not been hampered by his preconceived notion of a sort of difference in kind between Christianity and other traditions. Likewise, though Waite quite rightly rejects any application to the Grail legend of theories that make appeal to so-called 'gods of vegetation', it is regrettable that he should be much less clear about the ancient mysteries, which never had anything in common with this quite recently invented 'naturalism'; 'gods of vegetation' and other such fictions have never existed save in the imagination of Fraser[6] and others of his ilk whose anti-traditional intentions are not in doubt.

It seems that Waite has been more or less influenced by a certain 'evolutionism', a tendency that clearly betrays itself when he declares that the origin of the legend is much less important than the form it eventually attained; and he seems to believe that there must have been, from the one to the other, a sort of progressive improvement. In reality, where something truly traditional is con-

---

5. This reference is presumably to Eugene Bournouf, French linguist, author of *La Vase sacrée,* who deciphered the ancient Avestan tongue using manuscripts brought back by Anquetil-Duperron. ED.

6. Sir James G. Fraser, author of *The Golden Bough.* ED.

cerned, everything must on the contrary be present from the beginning, and subsequent developments serve only to render it more
explicit without the adjunction of new and external elements. Waite
seems to admit a sort of 'spiritualization' whereby a higher meaning
might be grafted on to something that did not originally possess it—
whereas it is in fact usually the other way round—in this way recalling a bit too closely the profane outlook of the 'historians of
religion'. We find a striking example of this sort of reversal in connection with alchemy, for Waite thinks that material alchemy preceded spiritual alchemy, and that this latter made its appearance
only with Khunrath and Jacob Boehme. If he had been familiar with
certain Arabic treatises extant well before these writers he would
have been obliged to modify his opinion simply on the basis of written documents; moreover, since he recognizes that the language
employed is the same in both cases, we might ask him how he can be
sure in any given text that the operations described are material
only. The truth is that it was not always felt necessary to declare
explicitly that it was really a question of something else, something
that had to be veiled precisely by the symbolism then in use; and if
subsequently there were some who did declare this, it was largely
because of degenerations traceable to an ignorance of the value of
the symbols which led men to take everything literally and in an
exclusively material way, as did the 'puffers' who were the precursors
of modern chemistry. To think that a new meaning can be given to a
symbol that does not possess it intrinsically is almost to deny symbolism, for it makes of the latter something artificial if not entirely
arbitrary, and in any case something purely human. In this order of
ideas, Waite goes so far as to say that everyone finds in a symbol what
he himself puts into it, so that its meaning would change with the
mentality of each epoch; here we recognize the 'psychological' theories so dear to many of our contemporaries. Were we not right, then,
to speak of 'evolutionism'? We have said it often but cannot repeat it
often enough: every true symbol bears its multiple meanings within
itself, and this from its very origin, because it is not constituted as
such by any human convention but in virtue of the 'law of correspondence' that links all worlds together; if some see these meanings
while others do not, or see them only in part, they are no less truly

contained in the symbol, for it is the 'intellectual horizon' of each person that makes all the difference, symbolism being an exact science and not a reverie in which individual fantasies are given free rein.

In matters of this order, then, we do not believe in the 'poetic inventions' of which Waite seems disposed to make so much; far from transmitting the essential, these inventions merely hide it, intentionally or not, by wrapping it in a 'fiction' of misleading appearances that sometimes conceal it only too well, for when they encroach overmuch it finally becomes nearly impossible to discover the deep and original meaning. Is this not how symbolism among the Greeks degenerated into 'mythology'? This danger is most to be feared when the poet himself is unaware of the real value of symbols, for it is evident that such cases do occur (the fable of the 'ass bearing relics' applies here as well as to many other situations), the poet then playing a part analogous to that of the common people when they conserve and unwittingly transmit initiatic teaching, as we have just said above. A question arises here most particularly: were the authors of the Grail romances poets of this latter kind, or were they on the contrary conscious to some degree of the profound meaning they were expressing? It is, of course, not easy to answer this with any certainty, for here again appearances can be deceiving. Faced with a mixture of insignificant and incoherent elements, one is tempted to think that the author did not know what he was speaking about; yet this need not necessarily be so, for it often happens that the obscurities and even the contradictions are quite intentional, and that pointless details are expressly included to lead the profane astray in the same way that a symbol may be deliberately concealed within a more or less complicated ornamental pattern; in the Middle Ages, especially, examples of this kind abound; one need only look at Dante and the Fedeli d'Amore. The fact that the higher meaning is less transparent in the work of Chrétien de Troyes, for example, than in that of Robert de Boron, does not necessarily prove that the first was less conscious of it than the second; still less should we conclude that this meaning is absent from his writings, which would be an error comparable to attributing to the ancient alchemists preoccupations of a merely material order for the sole reason that they did not deem it opportune to spell out in so many words that their science was in reality of a spiritual nature.[7] Further-more, the question of the 'initiation' of the authors of the romances is perhaps less important than we might first think, for it makes no difference in any case to the external forms under which the subject is presented; once we are dealing with an 'exteriorization', but not in any way a 'vulgarization', of esoteric teaching, it is easy to under-stand that the form must be as it is. We would go further and say that even a profane person may serve as 'spokesman' [*porte-parole*] of an initiatic organization engaged in such an 'exteriorization', in which case he will have been chosen simply for his qualities as a poet or writer, or for some other contingent reason. Dante wrote in full knowledge of what he was doing; Chrétien de Troyes, Robert de Boron, and many others were probably less conscious of what they were expressing, and some among them probably understood noth-ing at all; but ultimately this is of no importance, for if there was an initiatic organization behind them, whatever it may have been, the danger of a deformation due to their incomprehension was thereby averted since this organization was able to guide them continually without their even suspecting it, either through the intermediary of certain of its members who furnished them with the elements to be put into their work, or through suggestions or influences of another kind, more subtle and less 'tangible' but no less real for all that, nor less effective. It will easily be seen that this has nothing to do with so-called poetic 'inspiration' as the moderns understand the term and which is only imagination pure and simple, or with 'literature' in the profane sense of the word; neither, for that matter, let us has-ten to add, is it a question of 'mysticism', but this last point bears directly on other questions to be considered in the second part of this study.

It seems beyond doubt that the origins of the Grail legend must be linked to the transmission from Druidism to Christianity of tra-ditional elements of an initiatic order. Once this transmission had

7. If Waite believes, as he seems to, that certain things are too 'material' to be compatible with the existence of a higher meaning in the texts where they appear, one might ask him what he thinks, for example, of Rabelais and Boccaccio.

been effected in a regular manner, whatever the modalities of that transmission may have been, these elements thereby became an integral part of Christian esoterism. We are in agreement with Waite on this second point, but must say that the first seems to have escaped him. There can be no doubt of the existence of Christian esoterism in the Middle Ages; proofs of all kinds are ready to hand, and denials of it due to modern incomprehension, whether from the side of partisans or of adversaries of Christianity, are impotent in face of this fact, a point we have made often enough and which we need not insist upon again here. But even among those who do admit the existence of this esoterism there are many who have a more or less inexact conception of it; such seems to be the case with Waite, judging from his conclusions, for here again we find confusions and misunderstandings that must be dispelled.

We say quite deliberately 'Christian esoterism', and not 'esoteric Christianity', for we are not in fact dealing with a special form of Christianity but with the 'inner' aspect of the Christian tradition; and it should be clear that this is more than a simple nuance of language. Besides, when there is reason to distinguish in this way two aspects of a traditional form, one esoteric and the other exoteric, it must be understood that they do not refer to the same domain, so much so that there can be no conflict or opposition of any sort between them. In particular, when the exoterism has a specifically religious character, as is the case here, the corresponding esoterism, while taking its base and support from the religious form, has nothing to do with the religious domain in and of itself, being situated in fact in an altogether different order. It follows immediately that esoterism can under no circumstances be represented by 'churches' or 'sects' of any kind, for these are always religious by definition, and therefore exoteric—yet another point we have dealt with elsewhere, and need only recall in passing. Certain 'sects' may indeed have been born of a confusion between the two domains, and from an erroneous 'exteriorization' of poorly understood and wrongly applied esoteric teaching; but true initiatic organizations, strictly keeping to their own proper domain, necessarily remain foreign to such deviations, and their very 'regularity' obliges them to recognize only what has the character of orthodoxy, even if this is only in the exoteric order. One may therefore be assured that those who persist in ascribing to 'sects' what concerns esoterism or initiation are on the wrong track and can only go astray. There is no need to make a fuller examination in order to rule out all hypotheses of this kind; and if one finds in some 'sects' elements that seem to be esoteric in nature, the conclusion to be drawn is not that these elements originated with these sects, but that, on the contrary, it was precisely with the sects that they were diverted from their true meaning.

Having established this point, certain apparent difficulties are at once resolved, or, more accurately, become non-existent; and thus there is no cause to wonder what the position of orthodox Christianity, understood in the ordinary sense, might be in respect to a line of transmission outside of the 'apostolic succession', such as is suggested in several versions of the Grail legend. If here it is a question of an initiatic hierarchy, then the religious hierarchy could not in any way be affected by its existence, which, moreover, it need not even acknowledge 'officially' so to speak since it exercises a legitimate jurisdiction only in the exoteric domain. Similarly, when there is question of a secret formula in relation to certain rites, we will say quite frankly that there is a singular naiveté in asking whether the loss or the omission of this formula may not prevent the celebration of the Mass from being regarded as valid. The Mass, as it exists, is a religious rite, and the other is an initiatic rite; each is valid in its own domain, and even if they share a 'eucharistic' character this does nothing to change the essential distinction, any more than the fact that one and the same symbol may be interpreted according to the esoteric and the exoteric points of view prevents these latter from being completely distinct and related to entirely different domains. Whatever may be the external resemblances, which, moreover, are due to correspondences between them, the import and aim of initiatic rites is altogether different from those of religious rites. With all the greater reason, then, there can be no point in trying to establish whether or not the mysterious formula in question might not be identified with a formula used in some church that possesses a more or less special ritual: firstly, as far as churches with a claim to orthodoxy are concerned, the variants of the ritual are completely secondary and have no bearing whatsoever on anything essential; secondly, these variant rituals can never be other than religious, and as such they are all perfectly equivalent, and consideration of one or another of them brings us no closer to the initiatic point of view. How much futile research and discussion could be avoided if one were clear from the outset on the principles involved!

Now, even if the writings on the Grail legend emanated directly or indirectly from an initiatic organization, this by no means implies that they constitute an initiatic ritual, as some have assumed rather bizarrely; and it is curious that, at least to our knowledge, no such hypothesis has ever been put forward with regard to works that describe an esoteric process quite openly, such as the *Divine Comedy* or the *Romance of the Rose*. It is in any case obvious enough that not all writings that present an esoteric character are for that reason rituals. Waite, who rejects this supposition with good reason, brings into clear relief some of the improbabilities it involves, notably that the supposed candidate for initiation would have to ask a question, rather than answer questions put by the initiator, as is generally the case; and we might add that the divergences among the different versions of the legend are incompatible with the character of a ritual, which necessarily has a fixed and definite form. But what in all this prevents the legend from being attached in some other respect to what Waite calls 'Instituted Mysteries', and which we would simply call initiatic organizations? Waite's objection derives from the fact that his notion of such organizations is far too narrow and inexact in more than one respect. On the one hand, he seems to conceive of them as something almost exclusively 'ceremonial' (a rather typically Anglo-Saxon way of seeing things, be it said in passing); on the other hand, falling victim to a very widespread error to which we have often called attention, he imagines them more or less as 'societies', whereas if some of them may have assumed this form it can only have been the result of an altogether modern degeneration. He has no doubt been personally acquainted with a good number of these pseudo-initiatic associations which are now rife throughout the West; and though they seem to have left him somewhat disaffected, he has nonetheless remained to some extent influenced by them, by which we mean that, failing to perceive clearly the difference between authentic initiation and pseudo-initiation, he wrongly attributes to genuinely initiatic organizations features comparable to those found in the counterfeit bodies with which he happened to come in contact; and this mistake entails still other consequences, which, as we shall see, bear directly on the positive conclusions of his book.

It should be obvious enough that nothing in the initiatic order could be confined in so narrow a framework as that offered by modern 'societies'; but it is precisely in failing to find anything remotely resembling his 'societies' that Waite finds himself at a loss and ends up endorsing the fantastic supposition that an initiation could exist outside of any organization or regular transmission. We can do no better here than to refer the reader to articles we have previously devoted to this question.[8] Outside these so-called 'societies' Waite apparently sees no other possibility than that of some vague and indefinite thing that he calls the 'secret church' or the 'interior church', following terminology, borrowed from such mystics as Eckarthausen and Lopukhin,[9] in which the very word 'church' indicates that one finds oneself reduced purely and simply to the religious point of view, even though it may be one of those more or less aberrant varieties in which mysticism tends to develop spontaneously as soon as it escapes the control of a rigorous orthodoxy. Waite in fact remains one of those—unfortunately so numerous today—who for various reasons confuse mysticism and initiation, and he goes so far as to speak indiscriminately of these two things, incompatible as they are, as though they were almost synonymous. For him, initiation ultimately resolves into nothing more than 'mystical experience'; and we even wonder whether fundamentally he does not conceive of this 'experience' as something 'psychological', which would again bring us back to a level inferior to that of mysticism

---

8. See *Perspectives on Initiation*, chaps. 26 and 27. ED.

9. The German mystic Karl von Eckartshausen (1752–1813), whose best known works are *God is Purest Love* and *The Cloud upon the Sanctuary*; and the less well known Russian mystic Ivan Vladimirovitch Lopukhin (1756–1812), whose writings on the 'Interior Church' are very scarce. See Waite's lengthy introduction to Lopukhin's *Some Characteristics of the Interior Church* (London: The Theosophical Publishing Company, 1912), and also chapter VII of Book XI of his *The Holy Grail*, cited at the beginning of this chapter. ED.

properly understood, because true mystical states elude the domain of psychology entirely, despite all the modern theories of the sort of which William James is the best-known representative. As for the inner states, of which the realization pertains to the initiatic domain, they are neither psychological nor even mystical; they are something much more profound, and are not something of which one can neither say exactly what they are nor whence they come, since they imply on the contrary an exact knowledge and a precise technique, sentimentality and imagination no longer playing the least part here. To transpose truths of the religious order into the initiatic order is by no means to dissolve them into some hazy sort of 'ideal'; on the contrary, it is at once to penetrate both their deepest and their most 'concrete' [*positif*] meaning, dispelling the clouds that impede and limit the intellectual horizon of ordinary humanity. In truth, such a conception as Waite's no longer entails transposition, but at the very most a sort of prolongation, as it were, or an extension in the 'horizontal' sense, since whatever pertains to mysticism remains in the religious domain and does not extend beyond it; to go further requires more than adherence to a 'church' qualified as 'interior', primarily because such a 'church' is merely 'ideal', which, put more plainly, comes down to saying that it is in fact only an imaginary organization.

The 'secret of the Holy Grail' could not really be anything like this, nor could any other truly initiatic secret; if we would discover where this secret is found we must refer to the perfectly 'concrete' constitution of spiritual centers, something we have indicated quite explicitly in our study *The King of the World*. Here we shall confine ourselves to observing that Waite sometimes touches on matters of which the full significance seems to escape him: thus he speaks on various occasions of 'substitutes', which can be spoken words or symbolic objects; now this may refer either to the various secondary centers insofar as they are the images or reflections of the supreme center, or to successive phases of the 'obscuration' that gradually occurs in the external manifestations of these same centers in conformity with cyclical laws. Moreover, the first of these two cases is included in a way in the latter because the very formation of the secondary centers that correspond to particular traditional forms, whatever these may be, already marks the first degree of obscuration vis-à-vis the primordial tradition; in fact, from this point on the supreme center is no longer in direct contact with the outside world, and the link is only maintained through the intermediary of the secondary centers. On the other hand, if one of these should disappear, it can be said that it has in some way been resorbed into the supreme center, of which it was only an emanation. Here again there are degrees to be observed; it may happen that such a center only becomes more hidden and closed, and this is represented by the same symbolism as its complete disappearance, since any move away from the exterior is at the same time and in equal measure a return toward the Principle. We are alluding here to the symbolism of the final disappearance of the Grail: whether raised up to heaven, as in certain versions, or transported to the 'Kingdom of Prester John', as in certain others, exactly the same thing is signified, a point which Waite scarcely seems to suspect.[10] What is involved is this same withdrawal from the exterior toward the interior by reason of the state of the world at a certain time, or, to be more precise, the state of that portion of the world connected with the traditional form under consideration. This withdrawal, moreover, applies here only to the esoteric aspect of the tradition, the exoteric aspect having apparently remained unchanged in the case of Christianity; but it is precisely through the esoteric aspect that effective and conscious links with the supreme center are established and maintained. It must necessarily be the case, however, that something from it subsists, even if invisibly, as long as this traditional form remains living; for it to be otherwise would amount to saying that the 'spirit' had entirely withdrawn, leaving only a dead body behind. It is said that the Grail was no longer seen as it was for-

10. From the fact that a letter attributed to Prester John is obviously apocryphal, Waite draws the conclusion that he did not exist, a singular style of argument to say the least; and the question of linkages between the Grail legend and the Order of the Temple he treats in a scarcely less summary fashion. It seems that he is, no doubt unconsciously, in some haste to brush aside these matters that are both so full of significance and so incompatible with his 'mysticism'; and, in a general way, the German versions of the legend seem to us to merit more consideration than he accords them.

merly, but it is not said that it can no longer be seen; accordingly it is always present, at least in principle, for those who are 'qualified', but in fact these have become more and more rare, to the point where they now constitute only a tiny exception; and since the time when the Rosicrucians are said to have withdrawn into Asia, whether this be understood literally or symbolically, what possibilities for an effective initiation could such qualified individuals still find open to them in the West?

9

The Sacred Heart
and the Legend of
the Holy Grail

In his article[1] Louis Charbonneau-Lassay very rightly points out
that the legend of the Holy Grail, written down in the twelfth century though originating much earlier—since in reality it is a Christian adaptation of some very ancient Celtic traditions—is
something belonging to what might be called the 'prehistory of the
Eucharistic Heart of Jesus'. The idea of this comparison had already
occurred to us when reading an earlier, and from our standpoint
extremely interesting, article entitled 'Le Coeur humain et la notion
du Coeur de Dieu dans la religion de l'ancienne Égypte',[2] from
which we cite the following passage: 'In hieroglyphics, a sacred writing wherein the image of the thing itself often represents the very
word that designates it, the heart was represented only by an
emblem, the *vase*. Is not the heart of man indeed the vase in which
his life is continually maintained by means of his blood?' It is this
vase, taken as a symbol of the heart and substituting for it in Egyptian ideography, that at once called to mind the Holy Grail, all the
more in that we also see here, beside its general symbolic meaning
(considered, moreover, under both its human and its divine
aspects), a special and much more direct relationship with the very
heart of Christ.

---

1. ['Iconographie ancienne du Coeur de Jésus'], *Regnabit*, June 1925.
2. Ibid., Nov. 1924. [Cf. Charbonneau-Lassay, *Le Bestiaire du Christ* (Paris: Des-
clée de Brouwer, 1940), chap. 10, p95. ED.]

Indeed, the Holy Grail is the cup that contains the precious blood of Christ, and which even contains it twice, since it was used first at the Last Supper and then by Joseph of Arimathea to collect the blood and water that flowed from the wound opened in the Redeemer's side by the centurion's lance. This cup is thus a kind of substitute for the heart of Christ as a receptacle of his blood; it takes its place so to speak, and becomes its symbolic equivalent; and in this connection is it not still more remarkable that the vase should already in ancient times have been an emblem of the heart? Moreover, the cup in one form or another, just as the heart itself, plays an important part in many of the traditions of antiquity, particularly so among the Celts no doubt, since the whole fabric of the legend of the Holy Grail, or at least its guiding thread, came from them. It is regrettable that we cannot know with any precision what form this tradition took prior to Christianity, and so it is for everything concerning the Celtic doctrines, for which oral teaching was the sole means of transmission; but there are enough concordances for us at least to establish the meanings of the principal symbols that figured in them, this after all being what is most essential.

But let us return to the legend in the form in which it has come down to us, since what it has to say of the Grail's origin is particularly worthy of our attention: the cup was fashioned by angels from an emerald that fell from Lucifer's brow at the time of his fall. This emerald is strikingly reminiscent of the *urnā*, the frontal pearl that in Hindu iconography often takes the place of the third eye of *Shiva*, representing what might be called the 'sense of eternity'. This comparison seems better suited than any other to clarify exactly the symbolism of the Grail; and it illustrates yet another relationship with the heart, which, for the Hindu tradition, as for many others— though perhaps in Hinduism more clearly so—is the center of the integral being, to which consequently this 'sense of eternity' must be directly attached.

It is then said that the Grail was entrusted to Adam in the Terrestrial Paradise, but that at the time of his fall Adam lost it in his turn, for he could not take it with him when he was cast out of Eden; and this also becomes very clear in light of what we have just indicated: man, separated from his original center through his own fault, found himself henceforth confined to the temporal sphere; he could no longer regain the unique point from which all things are contemplated under the aspect of eternity. The Terrestrial Paradise was in fact the true 'Center of the World', which is everywhere symbolically assimilated to the divine Heart; and can it not be said that as long as he lived in Eden Adam truly lived in the Heart of God?

What follows next is more enigmatic: Seth was able to return to the Terrestrial Paradise and was thus able to recover the precious vase. Now Seth is one of the figures of the Redeemer, the more so as his very name expresses the ideas of foundation and stability, and he announces in a way the restoration of the primordial order destroyed by the fall of man. From this point there was at least a partial restoration in the sense that Seth and those who possessed the Grail after him were able thereby to establish, somewhere on earth, a spiritual center that was like an image of the Lost Paradise. The legend does not say where or by whom the Grail was preserved up to the time of Christ, or how its transmission was assured; but its manifestly Celtic origin suggests that the Druids probably played a part here, and that they must be numbered among the regular guardians of the primordial tradition. In any case, the existence of such a spiritual center, or even of several centers, simultaneously or successively, does not seem to be in doubt, wherever we may suppose them to have been located. What should be noted is that, among other designations, 'Heart of the World' was always and everywhere applied to these centers, and that in all traditions the descriptions of these centers are based upon an identical symbolism which can be traced to the precise details. Is this not sufficient to show that the Grail, or what is represented as such, had, already prior to Christianity, and even for all time, a very close link with the divine Heart and with *Emmanuel*, that is to say with the manifestation, virtual or real according to the epoch concerned, but always present, of the Eternal Word at the heart of terrestrial humanity?[3]

According to the legend, after the death of Christ the Holy Grail was transported to Britain by Joseph of Arimathea and Nicodemus;

---

3. *Emmanuel* means 'with us [is] God [*El*]'. ED.

the story of the Knights of the Round Table and their exploits, which we do not intend to take up here, then begins to unfold. The Round Table was destined to receive the Grail upon one of its knights having succeeded in winning it and bringing it from Great Britain to Brittany; and this table is also probably a very ancient symbol, one of those associated with the idea of the spiritual centers to which we have just alluded. Moreover, the circular form of the table is related to the 'zodiacal circle' (another symbol that merits a special study) through the presence around it of twelve chief personages, a feature that is also to be found in the constitution of all the centers in question. This being so, may one not see in the number of the twelve apostles one sign among a multitude of others of the perfect conformity of Christianity with the primordial tradition, to which the designation 'pre-Christian' so precisely fits? And we have also noticed in connection with the Round Table a strange concordance in the symbolic revelations made to Marie des Vallées[4] in which there is mention of a 'round table of jasper that represents the Heart of Our Lord', while there is at the same time mention of 'a garden that is the Holy Sacrament of the altar,' which, with its 'four fountains of living water,' is mysteriously identified with the Terrestrial Paradise. Again, is this not a rather astonishing and unexpected confirmation of the relationships we have pointed out?

Naturally, we cannot pretend that these cursory observations constitute a thorough study of a subject so little known as this; for the moment we must confine ourselves to giving mere indications, fully realizing that at first sight these are likely to be something of a surprise to those unfamiliar with the ancient traditions and their customary modes of symbolic expression. But we intend to develop and justify them more amply later through articles in which we may be able to touch on many other points no less worthy of interest.[5]

Returning meanwhile to the legend of the Holy Grail, let us mention a singular complication that we have not yet taken into account.

---

4. See *Regnabit*, November 1924. [Marie des Vallées, a seventeenth-century nun, contemplative, and visionary, who was also the confidant and inspirer of St John Eudes, who himself was the apostle of public devotion to the Sacred Hearts of Jesus and Mary. ED.]

5. See *The King of the World*. ED.

The Sacred Heart and the Legend of the Holy Grail

Through one of those verbal assimilations that often play a far from negligible part in symbolism, and that may moreover have deeper reasons than we may imagine at first sight, the Grail is simultaneously a vase or cup (*grasale*) and a book (*gradale* or *graduale*). In some variants of the legend the two meanings are very closely linked, for the book becomes an inscription engraved by Christ or by an angel upon the cup itself. We do not intend to draw any conclusion from this at the moment, although parallels may easily be found with the 'Book of Life' and certain elements in Apocalyptic symbolism.

Let us also add that the legend associates the Grail with other objects, notably a lance, which, in the Christian adaptation, is none other than the lance of the centurion Longinus; but what is curious is that this lance, or one of its equivalents, already existed as a sort of complementary symbol for the cup in ancient traditions. Among the Greeks the spear of Achilles was credited with the power to cure the wounds it had caused; and medieval legend attributes precisely the same power to the lance of the Passion, recalling another similarity of the same kind: in the myth of Adonis (whose name, moreover, signifies 'the Lord'), when the hero is mortally gored by the tusk of a wild boar (which here replaces the lance), his blood, flowing to the earth, gives rise to a flower.[6] Now, Charbonneau-Lassay has pointed to 'a twelfth-century press-mould for altar bread on which the blood from the wounds of the Crucified can be seen falling in droplets that are transformed into roses, and a thirteenth-century stained glass window of the cathedral of Angers, in which the divine blood, flowing in rivulets, also blossoms into the shapes of roses.'[7] We shall return later to the topic of floral symbolism, viewed under a somewhat different aspect; but whatever may be the multiplicity of meanings presented by nearly all the symbols, they fit together in perfect harmony, and this very multiplicity, far from constituting a disadvantage or shortcoming, is on the contrary, for

6. On the symbolism of the wild boar and its 'polar' significance, which places it squarely in relation with the 'World Axis', see 'The Wild Boar and the Bear', in *Symbols of Sacred Science*, chap. 24.

7. *Regnabit*, January 1925.

89

anyone who can understand it, one of the chief advantages of a language far less narrowly limited than the ordinary.

By way of concluding these notes let us mention several symbols that sometimes take the place of the cup in various traditions and that are in fact identical with it. This is not to depart from our subject, for the Grail itself, as may easily be realized from everything we have just said, originally had no other significance than that generally attributed to the sacred vase or vessel, wherever it is encountered, notably the significance attributed in the East to the sacrificial cup containing the Vedic *Soma* (or the Mazdean *Haoma*), that extraordinary eucharistic 'prefiguration' to which we shall perhaps return on another occasion.[8] What the *Soma* properly represents is the 'draught of immortality' (the *Amrita* of the Hindus and the *Ambrosia* of the Greeks, two etymologically related words), which confers on or restores to those who receive it with the requisite disposition that 'sense of eternity' to which we have already referred.

One of the symbols that we wish to mention is the downward-pointing triangle, which is a kind of schematic representation of the sacrificial cup and is encountered as such in certain *yantras*, or geometrical symbols, in India. But what is also very remarkable from our point of view is that the same figure is also a symbol of the heart, the shape of which it reproduces in a simplified way, the 'triangle of the heart' being an expression current in all Eastern traditions. This leads to the interesting observation that the figure of a heart inscribed in a triangle thus oriented is in itself altogether legitimate, whether it be a question of the human heart or of the divine Heart, and that this is very significant when it is related to the emblems used by certain Christian Hermeticists of the Middle Ages, whose intentions were always fully orthodox. If in modern times some have sought to attach a blasphemous meaning to this figure,[9] it is because, consciously or not, they have altered its primary sense to the point of reversing its normal value. This is a phenomenon for which many examples could be cited and which moreover finds its explanation in the fact that certain symbols are indeed susceptible of

8. See *The King of the World*, chap. 6. ED.
9. *Regnabit*, August–September 1924.

a twofold interpretation and have, as it were, two opposing faces. For example, do not the serpent and the lion both signify, according to context, Christ and Satan? We cannot set forth here a general theory on this subject, for this would lead us too far afield, but it goes without saying that in all this there is something that makes the handling of symbols a very delicate business and that also calls for quite special care when it comes to discovering the real meaning of certain emblems and of correctly interpreting them.

Another symbolism that is frequently equivalent to the cup is that of flowers: does not the form of a flower indeed evoke the idea of a 'receptacle', and do we not speak of the 'calyx' of a flower?[10] In the East, the symbolic flower par excellence is the lotus; in the West, the rose most often plays the same role. We do not of course mean to imply that this is the only significance proper to the rose, or to the lotus; quite the contrary, for we have ourselves just pointed out another, but we willingly see this significance in the design embroidered on the altar canon at the abbey of Fontevrault,[11] where the rose is placed at the foot of a lance along which flow drops of blood. There this rose appears in association with the lance exactly as does the cup elsewhere, and it does seem to be collecting the drops of blood rather than developing from a transformation of one of them. Even so, the two meanings complement far more than they oppose each other, for in falling on the rose these drops of blood vivify it and make it bloom. They are the 'celestial dew', according to the expression so often used in reference to the idea of the Redemption or to the associated ideas of regeneration and resurrection; but that again would call for lengthy explanations even if we were to limit ourselves to bringing out the concordance of the various traditions in the case of this one other symbol.

On another front, since the Rose-Cross has been mentioned in connection with the seal of Luther,[12] we will say that this Hermetic emblem was at first specifically Christian, whatever may be the false and more or less 'naturalistic' interpretations given it from the sev-

10. The French *calice* can mean chalice, cup, or the calyx of a flower. ED.
11. *Regnabit*, January 1925, figure p106. ED.
12. Ibid., January 1925.

enteenth century onward, and is it not remarkable that in this figure the rose occupies the center of the cross, the very place of the Sacred Heart? Apart from those representations where the five wounds of the Crucified are figured as so many roses, the central rose, when it stands alone, can very well be identified with the Heart itself, with the vase that contains the blood, which is the center of life and also the center of the entire being.

There is still at least one other symbolic equivalent of the cup, the lunar crescent; but to explain this adequately would demand further elaborations quite outside the scope of the present study. We only mention it therefore in order not to neglect entirely any aspect of the question.

From all the comparisons brought forward above we can already draw one conclusion which we hope to be able to further clarify in the future: when one finds such concordances everywhere, is this not more than a mere indication of the existence of a primordial tradition? And how is it to be explained that even those who feel obliged in principle to admit that this primordial tradition exists think no more about it more often than not, and in fact go on reasoning as if it had never existed, or at least as if nothing of it had been preserved over the centuries? Some reflection on how abnormal such an attitude is will perhaps render one less disposed to wonder at certain considerations which, in truth, only seem strange by virtue of the mental habits of our time. Besides, only a little unprejudiced research is required to discover on all sides the signs of this essential doctrinal unity, a consciousness of which may sometimes have been obscured among mankind but has never entirely disappeared. And in proportion as one advances in this research, the more the points of comparison seem to multiply of their own accord and new proofs to appear at every turn: to be sure, the *Quaerite et invenietis* [Seek and ye shall find] of the Gospel is no vain saying.

Addendum

We will add a few words here[13] in answer to an objection that was made to our view of the relationship between the Holy Grail and the Sacred Heart, even though the reply already given at the time seems to us fully satisfactory.[14]

It is of little importance that Chrétien de Troyes and Robert de Boron did not see in the ancient legend, of which they were only the adapters, all the significance contained in it. This significance was nevertheless really there, and we claim only to have made it explicit without introducing anything 'modern' into our interpretation. It is quite difficult, moreover, to say exactly what the writers of the

13. This additional text was published in *Regnabit*, December 1925, and has been appended here in view of its relevance to the present chapter. ED.

14. See *Regnabit*, Oct. 1925, pp358–359. A correspondent had written to the journal: 'A very interesting study of René Guénon on the Holy Grail and the Heart of Jesus. But cannot one level against his thesis an objection that would undermine it to the point of collapse? Chrétien de Troyes probably never thought of the Heart of Christ. In any case, the Celts of ancient Gaul certainly never thought of it. To see in the Holy Grail an emblem of the Heart of Christ is therefore a quite modern interpretation, which may be ingenious but which would have astonished our ancestors!' *Regnabit* responded: 'Some day Guénon himself may be able to tell us what he thinks of the objection advanced against his thesis. We simply note that the complete "nescience" of the Celts or of Chrétien de Troyes concerning the Heart of Jesus cannot "undermine" the interpretation of the legend of the Holy Grail given us by Guénon. He does not assert that the Celts *have seen* in the mysterious Vase an emblem of the Heart of Jesus. He shows that the Holy Grail—which the Celts knew, and the legend of which they passed on to us—is *objectively* an emblem of the living Heart, which is the true cup and the true life. Now this second affirmation is independent of the first. That the Celts *did not see* such and such a meaning in the legend that nourished their thought does not prove that this meaning is absent. It simply proves that this meaning remains hidden, even to those who must have loved the admirable legend so much. Today we all know that the phrase *full of grace* of the angelic salutation includes the grace of the Immaculate Conception of Mary. Imagine that during long centuries an entire school of theology *had not seen* in the formula the meaning that we see today—this would not prove that the meaning *is not there*. It would prove simply that this school had not grasped the entire significance of the formula. It is *a fortiori* possible that one of the true meanings of a religious myth may not have been perceived even by those who piously conserved the legend.' ED.

twelfth century saw or did not see in the legend; and given that they only played the part of 'transmitters', we readily agree that they did not see all that was seen by those who inspired them, that is, the real custodians of the traditional doctrine.

On the other hand, as regards the Celts, we were careful to recall the precautions that are necessary when speaking of them in the absence of any written documents. But why should it be supposed, despite the contra-indications that are nevertheless available, that the Celts were less favored than the other ancient peoples? We see everywhere, and not only in Egypt, the symbolic assimilation of the heart and the cup or vase. Everywhere the heart is considered to be the center of the being, a center that in the many aspects of this symbol is both divine and human. Furthermore, the sacrificial cup everywhere represents the Center or the Heart of the World, the 'abode of immortality'.[15] What more is required? We are well aware that the cup and the lance, or their equivalents, have had yet other meanings, in addition to those we mentioned, but without wishing to dwell any further on this point, we can say that all these meanings, no matter how strange some of them may appear to modern eyes, are in perfect agreement among themselves, and that they really express applications of the same principle to diverse orders according to a law of correspondence on which is founded the harmonious multiplicity of meanings included in all symbolism.

We hope to show in other studies not only that the Center of the World is in fact to be identified with the Heart of Christ, but also that this identity was plainly indicated in ancient doctrines. Obviously, the expression 'Heart of Christ' must in this case be taken in a sense that does not coincide precisely with that which could be

---

15. We could have recalled the Hermetic *athanor*, the vase where the 'Great Work' is effected, the name of which, according to some, was derived from the Greek *athanatos*, 'immortal'. The invisible fire that is perpetually maintained there corresponds to the vital heat that resides in the heart. Likewise, we could have shown the relationships with another very widely used symbol, that of the *egg*, which signifies resurrection and immortality and to which we may have occasion to return. On the other hand, we note that the cup in the Tarot cards (the origin of which is quite mysterious) has been replaced by the heart in ordinary playing cards, which is another indication of the equivalence of the two symbols.

called 'historical', but it must be said yet again that historical facts themselves, like all the rest, are 'translations' of higher realities into their own particular 'language' and conform to the law of correspondence we have just alluded to, a law that alone makes possible the explanation of certain 'prefigurations'. It is a question, if you will, of the Christ-principle, that is, of the Word manifested at the central point of the Universe. But who would dare to maintain that the Eternal Word and Its historical, earthly, and human manifestation are not really one and the same Christ under different aspects? We touch here on the relationship between the temporal and the timeless, and perhaps it is not appropriate to dwell further on this, for these are precisely things that symbolism alone can express, in the measure that they are expressible. In any case, it is enough to know how to read the symbols in order to find in them all that we ourselves have found; but alas, in our age especially, not everyone knows how to read them.

PART III
The Esoterism of Dante

10

Apparent and
Hidden Meaning

O voi che avete gl'intelletti sani,
Mirate la dottrina che s'asconde
Sotto il velame delli versi strani!

With these words[1] Dante indicates quite explicitly that there is a
hidden and, properly speaking, doctrinal significance to his work,
whose external and apparent meaning is only a veil that must be
penetrated by those who would understand it. Elsewhere the poet
goes still further, declaring that all writings, and not only sacred
ones, can be understood and must be explained principally according to four levels of meaning: *si possono intendere e debbonsi sponere*
massimamente per quattro sensi.[2] It is evident moreover that these
diverse meanings cannot in any way neutralize or oppose each
other, but on the contrary must complete each other, harmonizing

---

1. *Inferno,* IX, 61–63. [All citations from *The Divine Comedy* in the text and
appended to notes are taken from John Ciardi's translation (New York: W.W.
Norton & Company, Inc., 1977). Emphasis is always Guénon's. In the Ciardi translation, the lines cited here are numbered 58–60. ED.]

> Men of sound intellect and probity,
> Weigh with good understanding what lies hidden
> Behind the veil of my strange allegory!

2. *Convivio,* t. II, chap. 1. 'They may be understood, and they must be explained
in four senses.'

like the parts within a whole or as constituent elements of one single synthesis.

There is thus no doubt whatsoever that the *Divine Comedy* in its entirety can be interpreted in several senses, for we have in this regard the testimony of its author, who is certainly better qualified than anyone else to inform us of his own intentions. The difficulty begins only when it comes to determining these different meanings, especially the highest or the most profound, and it is here that different points of view naturally arise among commentators. They all generally agree on recognizing beneath the literal meaning in poetic narrative a philosophical (or rather, philosophico-theological) meaning, and also a political and social one; however, counting the literal meaning, this still makes only three, and Dante advises us to look for a fourth meaning. What can it be? For us, it can only be a properly initiatic meaning, metaphysical in its essence, to which are related numerous facts, equally esoteric in character though not all of a purely metaphysical order. It is precisely owing to its esoteric character that this profounder level of meaning has completely escaped most commentators. Yet if one ignores it, or perhaps fails to recognize it, the other levels of meaning can themselves only be partially grasped, for this fourth, or initiatic, meaning stands to the others as their principle, in which their multiplicity is coordinated and unified.

Even those who have glimpsed the esoteric side of Dante's work have committed many mistakes with respect to its true nature, for they have usually lacked a real understanding of these things, and their interpretations have been affected by prejudices that they found impossible to lay aside. Thus it is that Rossetti and Aroux, who were among the first to point out the existence of this esoterism, could conclude that Dante was guilty of 'heresy', not realizing that they were mixing together considerations relating to altogether different domains; so that, although they knew certain things, there were many others they did not know, and which we shall attempt to point out without in any way claiming to give a complete exposition of a subject that indeed seems truly inexhaustible.

The question for Aroux was whether Dante was Catholic or Albigensian. For others it seems rather to be whether he was Christian or pagan.[3] For our part, we do not think that such a point of view is necessary, for true esoterism is something completely different from outward religion, and if it has some relationship with it, this can only be insofar as it finds a symbolic mode of expression in religious forms. Moreover, it matters little whether these forms be of this or that religion, since what is involved is the essential doctrinal unity concealed beneath their apparent diversity. This is why in the past initiates participated in all forms of worship, following the customs established in whatever country they happened to be. Dante also understood this fundamental unity, and for this reason, and not by virtue of any superficial 'syncretism', he employed indifferently a terminology borrowed from Christianity and Greco-Roman antiquity as circumstances required. Pure metaphysics is neither pagan nor Christian, but universal; the ancient mysteries were not paganism, but were superimposed upon it.[4] In the same way there were in the Middle Ages some organizations of an initiatic, and not religious, character, but which took Catholicism as their base. If Dante belonged to some of these organizations, which seems to us indisputable, this is no reason to declare him a 'heretic'. Those who think in this way give proof of a false or incomplete idea of the Middle Ages; they see only the outer aspect of things so to speak, because for all other aspects terms of comparison are no longer to be found in the modern world.

Such being the real character of all initiatic organizations, there were only two cases where an accusation of 'heresy' might have been leveled at some of them, or at least at some of their members, and this in order to conceal other grounds for complaint that were much more legitimate, but which could not be expressed openly. In the first case certain initiates indulged in inopportune disclosures, risking both a disturbance in minds as yet unprepared for knowledge of higher truths, and also provoking disorder at the social level. The

---

3. Cf. Arturo Reghini, 'L'Allegoria esoterica di Dante', in *Nuovo Patto*, September–November 1921, pp541–548.

4. We must say that we would prefer another word to 'paganism', which has been imposed by long usage but was originally only a term of contempt applied to the Greco-Roman religion in the last stage of its decadence, where it was reduced to the state of simple popular 'superstition'.

authors of such disclosures erred in creating a confusion of the esoteric and the exoteric orders, a confusion that sufficiently justified
the reproach of 'heresy'. This situation has arisen on a number of
occasions in Islam,[5] where, however, the esoteric schools do not
normally encounter any hostility at the hand of the religious and
judicial authorities representing exoterism. In the second case, the
same accusation was simply taken as a pretext by a political power to
destroy adversaries thought all the more formidable for being so
difficult to reach by ordinary means. The destruction of the Order of
the Temple is the most celebrated instance of this type, and this
event has a direct connection with the subject of the present study.

5. We make particular allusion to the celebrated example of Al-Ḥallāj, who was
put to death in Baghdad in the year 309 of the Hegira (AD 921), and whose memory
is venerated even by those who think he was justly condemned for his imprudent
disclosures.

11

The 'Fede Santa'

In the Vienna Museum are two medallions, one representing Dante and the other the painter Peter of Pisa; the reverse side of each bear the letters F.S.K.I.P.F.T., which Aroux interprets as: *Frater Sacrae Kadosch, Imperialis Principatus, Frater Templarius*. For the first three letters this interpretation is obviously incorrect and does not convey any intelligible meaning; we think it should read *Fidei Sanctae Kadosch*. The association of the *Fede Santa*, of which Dante seems to have been a leader, was a tertiary order of Templar filiation, justifying the name *Frater Templarius*; and its dignitaries bore the title of *Kadosch*, a Hebrew word meaning 'holy' or 'consecrated', which has been preserved to our days in the high grades of Masonry. It is then not without reason that Dante takes Saint Bernard, who established the rule of the Order of the Temple, as his guide for the completion of his own celestial journey,[1] apparently wishing to point out in this way that, given the conditions characteristic of his time, access to the highest possible degree of the spiritual hierarchy was attainable only in this way.

In order to explain the *Imperialis Principatus*, perhaps one need not limit oneself to considering Dante's political role, which shows that the organizations to which he belonged were at the time well disposed toward the imperial power. We must point out moreover that the 'Holy Empire' has a symbolic significance and that even today in Scottish Masonry the members of the Supreme Councils bear the titles of dignitaries of the Holy Empire, while the title

---

1. *Paradiso*, xxxi. The word *contemplante*, which Dante uses later to describe Saint Bernard (idem, xxxii, 1), appears to have a double meaning due to its affinity with the name of the *Temple* itself.

'Prince' appears in the denominations of many grades. Further-more, beginning with the sixteenth century the leaders of the differ-ent organizations of Rosicrucian origin bore the title of Imperator; and there are reasons to think that in Dante's time the *Fede Santa* bore certain similarities to what later became the 'Brotherhood of the Rose-Cross', even if the latter is not more or less directly derived from the former.

We shall find many more parallels of this kind, and Aroux himself indicated a considerable number of them. One of the essential points on which he shed light, without perhaps drawing from it all the conclusions it implies, is the significance of the different sym-bolic regions Dante describes, and more especially the 'heavens'. These regions actually represent as many different states, and the heavens are properly speaking 'spiritual hierarchies', that is to say degrees of initiation. In this context an interesting concordance could be established between the conception of Dante and that of Swedenborg, not to speak of certain theories of the Hebrew Kab-balah, and especially of Islamic esoterism. In this regard Dante him-self has provided a clue worth mentioning: *A vedere quello che per terzo cielo s'intende . . . dico che per* CIELO *intendo la scienza e per* CIELI *le scienze* [author's emphasis].[2] But what exactly are these 'sciences' understood under the symbolic designation of the 'heavens', and should we see therein an allusion to the 'seven liberal arts' so often mentioned elsewhere by Dante and his contemporaries? What leads us to think that this must be the case is that according to Aroux, 'the Cathars had signs of recognition, passwords, and astrological doc-trine as early as the twelfth century; they conducted their initiations at the vernal equinox; their scientific system was founded on the doctrine of correspondences: Grammar corresponded to the Moon, Dialectic to Mercury, Rhetoric to Venus, Music to Mars, Geometry to Jupiter, Astronomy to Saturn, and Arithmetic or Illumined Rea-son to the Sun.' Accordingly, to the seven planetary spheres—the first seven of Dante's nine heavens—corresponded the seven liberal arts respectively; and precisely these same designations are depicted

2. *Convivio*, t.II, chap. 14. 'To see what is meant by this third heaven, I say that by *heaven* I mean science, and by *heavens*, sciences.'

on the seven rungs of the left upright of the *Ladder of the Kadosch* (30th degree of Scottish Masonry). The ascending order, in this latter case, differs only in an inversion, on the one hand, of Rhetoric and Logic (which is substituted here for Dialectic), and, on the other, of Geometry and Music; and also in that the science corresponding to the Sun (Arithmetic) occupies the rank normally assigned to that star in the astrological order of the planets—the fourth, or midpoint of the septenary—whereas the *Cathars* placed it on the highest rung of their *Mystical Ladder*, as on the corresponding rung on the ladder's opposite upright, Dante places Faith (*Emounah*), that is to say this mysterious *Fede Santa* of which he was himself *Kadosch*.[3]

However, further comment is necessary on this subject, for how is it that correspondences of this kind, which are assimilated to real initiatic degrees, have been attributed to the liberal arts, which, after all, were taught publicly and officially in all the schools? We think they must have been considered in two ways, the one exoteric and the other esoteric. It is possible to superimpose on any profane science another science that is related to the same object but looks at it from a profounder point of view, and which is to that profane science what the higher meanings of the scriptures are to their literal meaning. One could say further that external sciences serve as a mode of expression for higher truths because they are themselves only the symbol of something that is of another order; for as Plato said, the perceptible is only a reflection of the intelligible. The phenomena of nature and the events of history all have a symbolic value in that they express something of the principles upon which they depend, and of which they are the more or less remote consequences. Thus, by means of a suitable transposition, all science and all art can assume a true esoteric value; why then, in the initiations of the Middle Ages, should the expressions drawn from the liberal arts not have played a role comparable to that played in speculative Masonry by language borrowed from the art of the builders? We will go further: to look at things in this way is, after all, to bring

---

3. Concerning the *Mysterious Ladder of the Kadosch* [the Holy Ones], which we shall consider later in this study, see the *Manuel maçonnique* of F∴ Vuilliaume, pl. xvi and pp 213–214. We cite the second edition (1830).

them back to their principle; this point of view is, therefore, inherent in their very essence, and not accidentally super-added; and if this is the case, could not the tradition to which it is connected go back to the very origin of the sciences and arts, whereas the exclusively profane viewpoint preponderant in the modern age would only be the result of a general forgetfulness of this tradition? We cannot deal with this question and its many ramifications here, but let us see how Dante himself, in the commentary he gives on his first *Canzone*, points out the way in which he applies to his own work the principles of some of the liberal arts: *O uomini, che vedere non potete la sentenza di questa Canzone, non la rifiutate però; ma ponete mente alla sua bellezza, che è grande, sì per* COSTRUZIONE, *la quale si pertiene alli* GRAMMATICI; *sì per* L'ORDINE DEL SERMONE, *che si pertiene alli* RETTORICI; *si per lo* NUMERO DELLE SUE PARTI, *che si pertiene alli* MUSICI [author's emphasis].[4] Do we not hear an echo of the Pythagorean tradition in this way of relating music and number in a science of rhythm, with all its correspondences; and is it not this same tradition, precisely, that makes possible an understanding of the 'solar' role attributed to arithmetic, which it makes the common center of all the other sciences, and also of the correspondences that unite them, especially of music with geometry, through knowledge of proportion in forms (which finds its direct application in architecture), and, in the case of astronomy, through knowledge of the harmony of the celestial spheres? In what follows we shall see clearly enough what fundamental importance the symbolism of numbers assumes in Dante's work; and even if this symbolism is not uniquely Pythagorean and reappears in other doctrines for the simple reason that truth is one, it is no less permissible to think that from Pythagoras to Virgil, and from Virgil to Dante, the 'chain of the tradition' was undoubtedly unbroken on Italian soil.

---

4. Here is the translation of this text: 'O men, who cannot see the meaning of this Song, do not however reject it; but pay attention to its beauty, which is great, either for its *construction*, which concerns the *grammarians*; or for the *order of its discourse*, which concerns the *rhetoricians*; or for the *number of its parts*, which concerns the *musicians*.'

12

Masonic and
Hermetic Parallels

From the general observations made thus far we must now return
to the following rather remarkable parallels pointed out by Aroux,
and to which we alluded above:[1]

Hell represents the *profane world, Purgatory* is the place of *initiatic trials,* and *Heaven* is the abode of the *Perfect Ones,* where
we find intelligence and love combined and raised to their
zenith.... The celestial circle described by Dante[2] begins with
the *alti Serafini,* who are the *Principi celesti,* and ends at the lowest ranks of Heaven. Now it happens that certain lower dignitaries of Scottish Masonry (which claims to go back to the
Templars, and of which Zerbino, the Scottish prince and Isabelle
of Galicia's lover, is the personification in Ariosto's *Orlando Furioso*) are also called princes, *Princes of Mercy*; that their assembly
or chapter is called the *Third Heaven*; that they have a *Palladium,*
or statue of *Truth,* as their symbol, which, like Beatrice, is

---

1. We cite the summary of Aroux's works given by Paul Sédir [1871–1926], *Histoire des Rose-Croix,* pp16–20; second edition, pp13–17 [(Paris: Collection des hérmetistes, 1910); another book by Sédir, with the similar title of *Histoire et doctrines du Rose-Croix,* was published in Bihorel-lez Rouen by A.-L. Legrand, 1932]. The titles of these works by [Eugene] Aroux [1793–1859] are: *Dante hérétique, revolutionnaire et socialiste; revelations d'un catholique sur le moyen age* (Paris: J. Renouard, 1854; also, Paris: Éditions Niclaus, 1939), and *La Comédie de Dante, traduite en vers selon la lettre et commentée selon l'esprit, suivie de la Clef du langage symbolique des Fidèles d'Amour* (Paris: Heritiers J. Renouard, 1856–1857).

2. *Paradiso,* VIII.

adorned in the three colors *green, white,* and *red;*[3] that their Worshipful Master (whose title is *Most Excellent Prince*), carrying an arrow in his hand and a heart within a triangle on his chest,[4] is a personification of *Love;* and that the mysterious number *nine,* 'by which Beatrice is especially loved'—Beatrice, 'who must be called Love' as Dante says in the *Vita Nuova*—is also assigned to this Worshipful Master, who is surrounded by nine columns and nine torches (each with nine branches and nine lights), and whose age, finally, is eighty-one years, a multiple (or more precisely the square) of nine, Beatrice being said to have died in the eighty-first year of the century.[5]

This *Prince of Mercy,* or *Scottish Trinitarian,* grade, is the 26th of the Scottish Rite. Here is what the F∴ Bouilly says about it in his *Explication des douze écussons* [*the 19th to the 30th*] *qui représentent les emblèmes et les symboles des douze grades philosophiques du Rite Ecossais dit Ancien et Accepté:*

This grade is, in our opinion, the most inextricable of all those that compose this learned category: it is also given the name *Scottish Trinitarian.*[6] Indeed, everything in this allegory offers the emblem of the Trinity: the background of three colors [green, white, and red]; the representation of *Truth* at the bottom; and, finally, everywhere this indication of the *Great Work of Nature* [to the phases of which the three colors allude], of the constitutive elements of the metals [sulphur, mercury, and salt],[7] of their fusion and their separation [*solve et coagula*], in a word,

3. It is at least curious that these three colors have in modern times become the national colors of Italy; moreover, a Masonic origin is quite generally attributed to these colors, although it is rather difficult to know whence the idea could have been directly derived.

4. To these distinctive signs we must add a 'crown of golden arrow-heads'.

5. Cf. *Light on Masonry* [David Bernard (Utica: William Williams, 1829)], p250, and *Manuel maçonnique,* pp179–182.

6. We must admit that we do not see the connection that may exist between the complexity of this grade and its name.

7. The alchemical ternary is often likened to that of the constitutive elements of the human being: spirit, soul, and body.

of the science of mineral chemistry [or rather of alchemy] which was founded by *Hermes* among the Egyptians, and which gave such power and breadth to medicine [*spagyric*].[8] So true is it that the sciences that lead to happiness and freedom succeed one another and are classified in this admirable order, that it proves the Creator has furnished men with all that can ease their suffering and prolong their sojourn on earth.[9] It is principally in the number *three*, so well represented by the three angles of the *Delta*, which the Christians have made the flamboyant symbol of Divinity, and which goes back to the most remote times,[10] that the skilled observer discovers the primeval source of everything that strikes the mind, enriches the imagination, and gives a just appreciation of social equality.... Therefore, noble Knights, let us not cease to remain *Scottish Trinitarians*, to maintain and honor the number *three* as the emblem of all that constitutes the duties of man, and that at the same time reminds us of the cherished Trinity of our Order, engraved on the columns of our Temples: *Faith, Hope*, and *Charity*.[11]

What we should retain above all from this passage is that the grade concerned, like nearly all those of the same class, presents a clearly Hermetic meaning; and what we should particularly note in this

---

8. The words between brackets have been added to render the text more comprehensible.

9. In these last words we see a discreet allusion to the 'elixir of long life' of the alchemists. The preceding grade (25th), that of the *Knight of the Brazen Serpent*, was explained as 'including a part of the first degree of the *Egyptian Mysteries*, whence *medicine* and the *great art* of compounding remedies originated.'

10. The author no doubt wishes to say 'the symbolic use of which goes back to the most remote times,' for we cannot suppose that he wanted to assign a chronological origin to the number *three* itself.

11. The three colors of this grade are sometimes regarded as symbolizing, respectively, the three theological virtues: white representing Faith, green Hope, and red Charity (or Love). The insignia of this grade of *Prince of Mercy* are a red apron, in the middle of which is painted or embroidered a white and green triangle, and a ribbon of the three colors of the Order worn crosswise, from which is suspended as a jewel an equilateral triangle (or Delta) made of gold. (See *Manuel maçonnique*, p 181.)

regard is the connection of Hermeticism to the Orders of Chivalry.[12] This is not the place to investigate the historical origin of the high grades of Scottish Masonry or to discuss the controversial theory of their descent from the Templars; but, whether there has been a real and direct filiation or only a reconstitution, it is nonetheless certain that most of these grades, and also some found in other rites, seem to be vestiges of organizations that formerly existed independently,[13] and most notably of the ancient Orders of Chivalry, the foundation of which was bound up with the history of the Crusades, that is to say with an epoch when between East and West there existed not only hostile relations, as those who confine themselves to appearances believe, but also active intellectual exchanges, exchanges implemented above all through the mediation of these same Orders. Must we accept that the latter borrowed Hermetic material from the East and then assimilated it, or should we not rather think that from the outset these Orders possessed an esoterism of this kind, and that it was their own initiation that qualified them to enter into relations with the Easterners on this terrain? This again is a question we cannot claim to resolve; but the second hypothesis, though less often entertained than the first,[14] contains nothing implausible for those who recognize, throughout the Middle Ages, the existence of a strictly Western initiatic tradition; and what could further prompt us to accept it is that Orders founded later, which never had dealings with the East, also possessed Hermetic symbolism—for example, the *Golden Fleece*, the very name of

12. A high Mason who seems more versed in the quite modern and profane science called 'history of religions' than in true initiatic knowledge, the Count Goblet d'Alviella, believed he could give a Buddhist interpretation to this purely Hermetic and Christian grade, under the pretext that there is a certain resemblance between the titles *Prince of Mercy* and *Lord of Compassion*.

13. In fact there was an *Order of the Trinitarians* or *Order of Mercy*, which had as aim, at least outwardly, the ransoming of prisoners of war.

14. Some have gone so far as to attribute an exclusively Persian origin to the coat of arms, which has fairly close ties with Hermetic symbolism, whereas in reality the coat of arms has existed from antiquity among many peoples, Western as well as Eastern, and especially among the Celts.

which is the clearest possible allusion to this symbolism. However this may be, in Dante's time Hermeticism certainly existed in the Order of the Temple, as did knowledge of certain doctrines more definitely of Arab origin of which Dante himself seems not to have been ignorant either, and which were no doubt transmitted to him in this way also—a point we shall explain in due course.

Let us return however to the Masonic correspondences mentioned by Aroux, only a few of which we have considered so far. There are several degrees of Scottish Masonry for which Aroux believes he can see a perfect analogy with the nine heavens that Dante traverses with Beatrice. Here are the correspondences that he gives for the seven planetary heavens: to the Moon corresponds the *profane*, to Mercury the *Knight of the Sun* (28th), to Venus the *Prince of Mercy* (26th, green, white, and red), to the Sun the *Great Architect* (12th) or the *Noachite* (21st), to Mars the *Great Scot of the Order of Saint Andrew* or *Patriarch of the Crusades* (29th, red with a white cross), to Jupiter the *Knight of the White and Black Eagle* or *Kadosch* (30th), and to Saturn the *Golden Ladder* of the same *Kadosch*. In truth, some of these attributions seem doubtful to us, especially that of the first heaven as the abode of the profane, for the place of these latter can only be in the 'outer darkness', and in fact have we not already seen that it is hell that represents the profane world, while the different heavens (including that of the Moon) can be reached only after undergoing the initiatic trials of Purgatory? It is well known also that the sphere of the Moon has a special relationship to Limbo; but this is an altogether different aspect of its symbolism and must not be confused with that aspect according to which it is represented as the first heaven. In fact, the Moon is at once *Janua Coeli* and *Janua Inferni*, Diana and Hecate.[15] The ancients knew this very well, as did Dante, who could not have been so mistaken as to accord the profane a celestial abode, even the very lowest.

---

15. These two aspects also correspond to the two solstitial doors; there would be much to say on this symbolism, which the ancient Latins summarized in the figure of Janus. On the other hand, there are some distinctions to make between hell, Limbo, and the 'outer darkness' mentioned in the Gospel; but this would lead us too far afield, and would not affect the present point, which is only concerned in a general way with the separation of the profane world from the initiatic hierarchy.

What is far less debatable is the identification of the symbolic fig-ures seen by Dante: the cross in the heaven of Mars, the eagle in that of Jupiter, and the ladder in that of Saturn. The cross is assuredly related to that which, after having been the distinctive sign of the Orders of Chivalry, still serves as the emblem of several Masonic grades; and if it is placed in the sphere of Mars, is this not an allu-sion to the military character of these Orders, their obvious raison d'être, and to the role they played externally in the military expedi-tions of the Crusades?[16] As for the other two symbols, it is impossi-ble not to recognize in them those of the *Kadosch Templar*; and at the same time the eagle, which classical antiquity attributed to Jupi-ter, as did the Hindus to *Vishnu*,[17] was the emblem of the ancient Roman Empire (which calls to mind the presence of Trajan[18] in the eye of that eagle), and it has remained so for the Holy Empire. The heaven of Jupiter is the abode of the 'wise and just princes' (*Diligite justitiam, qui judicatis terram*),[19] a correspondence which, like all those Dante gave to the heavens, is wholly explained in terms of astrology; and the Hebrew name for the planet Jupiter is *Tsedek*, meaning 'just'. Of the ladder of the *Kadosch* we have already said that since the sphere of Saturn is situated immediately above that of Jupiter, we reach the foot of this ladder by Justice (*Tsedakah*), and its summit by Faith (*Emunah*). This symbol of the ladder seems to be of Chaldean origin and to have been brought to the West with the mysteries of Mithra; at that time it had seven rungs, each fash-ioned of a different metal according to the correspondence of the metals with the planets, and in biblical symbolism we find Jacob's

---

16. One can also note that the heaven of Mars is represented as the abode of the 'martyrs of religion'; there is even a kind of pun on the words *Marte* and *martiri*, of which one could find other examples elsewhere. Thus the hill of Montmartre was once the *Mount of Mars* before becoming the *Mount of the Martyrs*. Apropos of this let us note in passing a rather strange fact: the names of the three martyrs of Mont-martre, *Dionysos, Rusticus,* and *Eleutheros,* are all names of Bacchus. Moreover, Saint Denis, considered the first Bishop of Paris, is commonly identified with Saint Denys the Areopagite; and in Athens, the Areopagus was also the *Mount of Mars*.

17. The symbolism of the eagle in the different traditions would call for a quite special study of its own.

18. Trajan, Roman Emperor, AD 98–117. ED.

19. *Paradiso,* XVIII, 91–93. ['Love justice, you who judge the earth.']

112

ladder joining the earth to the heavens, which presents an identical meaning.[20]

'According to Dante, the eighth heaven of Paradise, the starry heaven (or the heaven of the fixed stars), is the *Heaven of the Rose-Cross*. There the *Perfect* are clad in white, and display a symbolism analogous to that of the *Knights of Heredom*;[21] they profess the "evangelical doctrine"—Luther's very own—as opposed to Roman Catholic doctrine.' Here Aroux's interpretation testifies to his frequent confusion of the domains of esoterism and exoterism: true esoterism must lie beyond the oppositions expressed in the outer movements agitating the profane world, and if such movements are sometimes created or invisibly directed by powerful initiatic organizations, one can say that the latter dominate these movements without being part of them, so as to exercise their influence equally upon each of the opposing parties. It is true that the Protestants, and especially the Lutherans, habitually use the word 'evangelical' to describe their own doctrine, and we know also that Luther's seal bore a cross in the center of a rose, and that the Rosicrucian organization, which revealed itself to the public in 1604 (and which Descartes sought vainly to contact), declared itself 'anti-papist'. But it must be said that at the beginning of the seventeenth century the Rosicrucians were already very outward and far removed from the original and genuine Brotherhood of the Rose-Cross, which never constituted a society in the proper sense of the word. As for Luther, he seems to have been only a kind of subordinate agent, no doubt scarcely conscious of the role he had to play. These various points,

20. It is not without interest to note further that Saint Peter Damien, with whom Dante converses in the heaven of Saturn, appears in the list (in great part legendary) of the *Imperatores Rosae-Crucis* given in the *Clypeum Veritatis* of Iranaeus Agnostus (1618).

21. The *Order of Heredom of Kilwinning* is the *Great Chapter* of the high grades attached to the *Great Royal Lodge of Edinburgh* and founded, according to tradition, by the king Robert Bruce (Thory, *Acta Latomorum*, vol. 1, p317). The English word *Heredom* (or *heirdom*) means 'heritage' (of the Templars); however, some people derive this name from the Hebrew *Harodim*, a title given to those who directed the workers employed in the construction of the Temple of Solomon. (Cf. our article on this subject in *Études Traditionnelles*, March 1948.)

moreover, have never been completely elucidated.

Be that as it may, the white robes of the *Elect*, or the *Perfect*, though obviously reminiscent of certain apocalyptic texts,[22] appear above all to allude to the dress of the Templars; and in this respect the following passage is particularly significant:

> Qual è colui che *tace e dicer vuole*,
> Mi trasse Beatrice, e disse: mira
> Quanto è *il convento delle bianche stole!*[23]

Moreover, this interpretation makes it possible to give a very precise meaning to the expression 'the holy militia' found a little further on in lines which seem to express discretely the transformation of Templarism, after its apparent destruction, into Rosicrucianism:[24]

> In forma dunque di *candida rosa*
> Mi si mostrava la *milizia santa*,
> Che nel suo sangue Cristo fece sposa.

To make better understood the symbolism involved in Aroux's last quotation, here is the description of the *Celestial Jerusalem* as it appears in the *Chapter of the Sovereign Princes Rosicrucian*, of the *Order of Heredom of Kilwinning* or the *Royal Order of Scotland*, also named *Knights of the Eagle and the Pelican*:

> In the rear [of the last room] there is a picture showing a mountain from which flows a river by whose bank grows a tree bearing twelve kinds of fruit. On the summit of the mountain stands a

---

22. Rev. 7:13–14.

23. *Paradiso*, xxx, 127–129. Concerning this passage, we note that the word 'convent' has remained in usage in Masonry to designate its great assemblies.

> I, yearning to speak and silent—Beatrice drew me,
> and said: 'Now see how many are in *the convent*
> *of the white robes....*

24. *Paradiso*, xxxi, 1–3. The final verse may refer to the symbolism of the red cross of the Templars.

> Then in the form of a *white rose*, the host
> of the *sacred soldiery* appeared to me,
> all those whom Christ in his own blood espoused.

plinth made of twelve precious stones laid in twelve tiers. On top of this plinth is a golden square, and on the face of each side are three angels, each angel bearing the name of one of the twelve tribes of Israel. In this square is a cross, at the center of which lies a lamb. [25]

Here we again find apocalyptic symbolism, and in what follows it will be shown to what extent the cyclical ideas to which it is related are intimately linked to the very plan of Dante's work.

In cantos xxiv and xxv of the *Paradiso*, we find the triple kiss of the *Rosicrucian Prince*, the pelican, the white tunics (the same as those of the elders in the *Apocalypse*), the sticks of sealing wax, and the three theological virtues of the Masonic Chapters (Faith, Hope, and Charity).[26] The symbolic flower of the Brotherhood of the Rose-Cross (the *Rosa candida* of cantos xxx and xxxi) has been adopted by the Church of Rome as the figure of the Mother of the Savior (*Rosa mystica* of the litanies), and by that of Toulouse (the Albigenses) as the mysterious emblem of the general assembly of the *Fedeli d'Amore*. These metaphors were already employed by the *Paulicians*, predecessors of the *Cathars* in the tenth and eleventh centuries.

We thought it useful to reproduce all these parallels, which are interesting and could no doubt be multiplied without difficulty, but one should not, except perhaps in the cases of the Templars and the original Brotherhood of the Rose-Cross, claim to draw overly firm conclusions with regard to a direct filiation of the different initiatic forms among which we thus ascertain a certain community of symbols. In fact, not only are the fundamentals of the doctrines always and everywhere the same, but in addition (which may seem more

25. *Manuel maçonnique*, pp143–144. Cf. Rev. 21.
26. In the Chapters of the Rosicrucians (18th degree Scottish), the names of the three theological virtues are associated, respectively, with the three terms of the motto 'Liberty, Equality, Fraternity'; one could also compare them with what are called 'the three principal pillars of the Temple' in the symbolic grades: 'Wisdom, Strength, Beauty'. To these same three virtues Dante links Saint Peter, Saint James, and Saint John, the three apostles who witnessed the transfiguration.

surprising at first sight) the particular modes of expression themselves often present a striking similarity, even in the case of traditions too remote in time or space to make plausible any immediate influence on each other. To find an effective link in such cases it would no doubt be necessary to go much further back in time than recorded history allows.

Some commentators who have studied the symbolism of Dante's work, such as Rossetti and Aroux, confine themselves to an aspect that we would qualify as external, by which is meant that they have stopped at what could readily be called ritualistic forms, that is, at forms which, for those who are incapable of going further, conceal rather than express their profounder meaning. And as has been very justly said,

it is natural that it should be thus, for to grasp and understand the allusions and the conventional or allegorical references, one must be acquainted with the object of the allusion or allegory; and in the present case this means an apprehension of the mystical experiences through which true initiation causes the *myste* and the *épopte* to pass. For anyone with some experience of this kind, there can be no doubt about the existence, in the *Divine Comedy* and the *Aeneid*, of a metaphysico-esoteric allegory that simultaneously veils and unveils the successive phases through which the consciousness of the initiate passes in order to attain immortality.[27]

27. Arturo Reghini, art. cit., pp545–546.

13

Dante and Rosicrucianism

The same reproach of insufficiency that we have leveled against Rosetti and Aroux can also be addressed to Eliphas Lévi, who, while asserting a relationship to the ancient mysteries, nonetheless saw above all a political or politico-religious application which, in our view, is only of secondary importance, and which is always wrong in supposing that properly initiatic organizations are directly engaged in outer activities. Here, in fact, is what the author says in his *History of Magic*:

> There have been many commentaries and studies on Dante's work, but nobody, as far as we know, has pointed out its true character. The work of the great Ghibelline is a declaration of war on the Papacy through the daring revelation of the mysteries. Dante's epic is Johannite[1] and gnostic; there is a bold application of the diagrams and numbers of the Kabbalah to Christian dogmas, and a secret negation of all that is uncompromising in these dogmas. His journey through the supernatural worlds is accomplished as an initiation into the mysteries of Eleusis and Thebes. It is Virgil who guides and protects him in the circles of the new Tartarus, as though Virgil, the sensitive and melancholic prophet of the destinies of the son of Pollio, were in the eyes of the Florentine poet the illegitimate but real father of the Christian epic.

---

1. Saint John is often considered the head of the *interior* Church, and according to certain conceptions, of which an indication can be found here, some want to oppose him in this respect to Saint Peter, head of the *exterior* Church; the truth is rather that their respective authority does not apply to the same domain.

Thanks to the pagan genius of Virgil, Dante escapes from this abyss on the door of which he had read a sentence of despair; he escapes *by putting his head in place of his feet and his feet in place of his head* (that is to say by taking the opposite view to dogma), and reascends to the light by making use of the devil himself as a monstrous ladder; he escapes the terrible by means of terror, the horrible by means of horror. Hell, it seems, is an impasse only for those who do not know to turn around. Dante rubs the devil the wrong way, if this common expression be permitted, and is set free by his audacity. This is already Protestantism surpassed, and the poet of Rome's enemies has already foreseen Faust rising to Heaven on the head of the vanquished Mephistopheles.[2]

In reality, the wish to 'reveal the mysteries' —supposing such a thing were even possible (which it is not, for there is no real mystery that is not inexpressible) —and the bias of taking 'the view opposite to dogma' or of consciously reversing the meaning and value of symbols, would not be the mark of a very high initiation. Fortunately, we do not see, for our part, any evidence of this in Dante, whose esoterism is on the contrary shrouded by a veil that is rather difficult to penetrate, while at the same time resting on strictly traditional foundations. To make him a precursor of Protestantism, and perhaps of the French Revolution as well, simply because he was an adversary of the papacy in the *political* arena, is to misunderstand his thought entirely or to understand nothing of the spirit of his time.

Something else that seems to us scarcely tenable is the belief that Dante was a 'Kabbalist' in the proper sense of the word. Here we are all the more inclined to be mistrustful, as we know only too well how some of our contemporaries readily delude themselves on this subject, thinking to have found elements of the Kabbalah wherever

---

2. This passage by Eliphas Lévi, like many others (taken mostly from *Dogme et Rituel de la Haute Magie*), was reproduced *verbatim* and with no indication of its provenance by Albert Pike [1809–1891] in his *Morals and Dogma of the Ancient and Accepted Scottish Rite of Freemasonry* [Washington, D.C.: L.H. Jenkins, 1962, and many earlier editions by various publishers], p 822, the very title of which moreover is obviously taken from the same source.

there is any kind of esoterism. Have we not seen a Masonic writer solemnly affirm that the *Kabbalah* and *Chivalry* are one and the same thing, and, lacking even the most elementary linguistic notions, that the two words have a common origin?[3] In view of such improbabilities, one will understand the necessity to be wary, and not to be satisfied with vague correspondences in order to make someone into a Kabbalist. Now the Kabbalah is essentially the Hebrew tradition,[4] and we have no proof that a Jewish influence was exerted directly on Dante.[5] What has given rise to such a belief is solely the use he makes of the science of numbers; but even if this science does really exist in the Hebrew Kabbalah, and hold a place therein of the utmost importance, it is nonetheless also found elsewhere.[6] Will it also be claimed under the same pretext that Pythagoras was a Kabbalist?[7] As we have already stated, in this regard it is rather more to Pythagorism than to the Kabbalah that one could link Dante, who quite probably knew from Judaism, above all, what Christianity had preserved from this source in its own doctrine.

'Let us also point out,' Eliphas Lévi goes on to say, 'that Dante's Hell is only a *negative Purgatory*. Let us explain: his Purgatory seems to have formed itself in his Hell as in a mold; it is like the lid or "stopper" as it were of the bottomless pit, and one can understand that in scaling Paradise, the Florentine Titan would like to dispatch

3. Charles Mathieu Limousin, *La Kabbale littérale occidentale: les 32 voies de la sagesse du 'Sefer Ietzirah' expliquées par l'alphabet latin* [Paris: Nouvelle revue, 1897].

4. The word itself means 'tradition' in Hebrew, and unless one writes in this language there is no reason to use it to designate every tradition indiscriminately.

5. One should however say that according to contemporary testimonies Dante had a sustained friendship with the well-educated Jew Immanuel ben Solomon ben Jekuthiel (1270–1330), himself a poet; but it is nonetheless true that we see no trace of specifically Jewish elements in the *Divine Comedy*, whereas Immanuel was himself inspired by the latter in one of his own works, despite the contrary opinion of Israël Zangwill, which the comparison of dates renders quite untenable. [Immanuel ben Solomon, or Immanuel ben Zifroni (also known as Manoello Giudeo or 'Immanuel the Jew'), thought to have lived from 1261 to sometime after 1328. The *Encyclopaedia Judaica* (1972), vol. 8, pp1295–98, confirms Guénon's assertion that Dante influenced this Hebrew poet, and not the other way around. ED.]

6. See *Traditional Forms and Cosmic Cycles*, pt 3, chap. 3. ED.

7. This opinion was put forward by Reuchlin. [Johannes Reuchlin (1455–1522), Christian Kabbalist. ED.]

Purgatory into Hell with a single kick.' This is true in a sense, since the Mount of Purgatory was formed in the southern hemisphere of material spewed from the bosom of the earth when the abyss was dug by Lucifer's fall; yet Hell has nine circles, which are like an inverted reflection of the nine heavens, while Purgatory has only seven, the symmetry therefore not being exact in all respects.

'His Heaven is composed of a series of kabbalistic circles divided by a cross like the pentacle of Ezekiel; at the center of this *cross* blooms a *rose*, and here we see the symbol of the Rosicrucians appearing for the first time, publicly revealed and almost categorically explained.' At about the same time, moreover, this very symbol also appeared, though perhaps not so clearly, in another famous poetic work, *The Romance of the Rose*. Eliphas Lévi thinks that '*The Romance of the Rose* and the *Divine Comedy* are opposite forms [it would be more correct to say complementary] of the same work: the initiation into independence of the spirit, the satirizing of all contemporary institutions and allegorical formulas of the grand secrets of the Society of the Rose-Cross,' which in truth did not yet bear this name and, moreover, we repeat, was never (but for some more or less deviant branches later) a 'society' constituted with all the outward forms that this word implies. On the other hand, 'independence of the spirit,' or, to put it better, intellectual independence, was not so exceptional a thing in the Middle Ages as the moderns usually imagine, and the monks themselves did not hesitate to express their frank criticisms, evidence of which can be discerned even in cathedral statuary. In all this there is nothing properly esoteric; the two works in question contain something far more profound.

Eliphas Lévi goes on: 'These important manifestations of occultism coincided with the time of the fall of the Templars, since Jean de Meung or Clopinel, contemporary with Dante's old age, flourished at the court of Philip the Fair during its finest years. This is a profound book that pretends to be trifling;[8] it is a revelation as learned

---

8. The same thing can be said of some of Rabelais' works in the sixteenth century, which also have an esoteric import that it would be interesting to study more closely.

as that of Apuleius on the mysteries of occultism. The rose of Flamel, that of Jean de Meung, and that of Dante, were born of the same bush.'[9]

On these lines we would only caution that the word 'occultism', invented by Eliphas Lévi himself, is hardly suitable to designate what pre-dated him, especially when one reflects on what contemporary occultism has become, which, in claiming to be a restoration of esoterism, has succeeded only in becoming a crude counterfeit of it because its leaders have never been in possession of true principles or of any genuine initiation. Eliphas Lévi would no doubt be the first to disavow his would-be successors, to whom he was certainly very much superior intellectually while at the same time he was nonetheless far from being as profound as he wished to appear, wrongly viewing everything through the mentality of an 1848 revolutionary. If we have spent some time discussing his opinions, it is because we know how great his influence has been, even upon those who scarcely understood him, and because we think it best to fix the limits within which his competence can be acknowledged; his principal shortcoming, which was that of his time, was to put social preoccupations in the foreground and to mix them indiscriminately with everything. In Dante's day one certainly knew better how to assign to each thing its proper place in the universal hierarchy.

What is of particular interest in this for the history of esoteric doctrines is the finding that several important manifestations of these doctrines coincided, within just a few years, with the destruction of the Order of the Temple. There is an unquestionable connection between these events, although it is rather difficult to determine it precisely. In the early years of the fourteenth century, and doubtless already in the course of the preceding century, there was thus, in France as well as in Italy, a secret tradition ('occult' if one likes, but not 'occultist'), the very one that later was to bear the

---

9. Eliphas Lévi, *Histoire de la Magie*, 1860, pp359–360. It is worth noting apropos of this that there exists an Italian adaptation of the *Romance of the Rose*, entitled *Il Fiore*, whose author, 'Ser Durante Fiorentino', appears to be none other than Dante himself, whose real name was, in fact, Durante, of which Dante is only an abbreviated form.

121

name of Rosicrucianism. The denomination *Fraternitas Rosae-Crucis* appears for the first time in 1374, or, according to some (notably Michael Maier),[10] in 1413; and the legend of *Christian Rosenkreuz*, the supposed founder whose name and life are purely symbolic, was perhaps fully formed only in the sixteenth century; but we have just seen that the Rose-Cross symbol is certainly much earlier.

This esoteric doctrine, whatever particular designation one may wish to give it—if it is necessary to do so at all—prior to its appearance as Rosicrucianism in the strict sense of the word, presented some characteristics that allow us to join it with what is generally called Hermeticism. The history of the Hermetic tradition is intimately linked to that of the Orders of Chivalry, and was preserved at the time in question by initiatic organizations such as the *Fede Santa* and the *Fedeli d'Amore*, as also by the *Massenie of the Holy Grail*. Of the latter the historian Henri Martin says,[11] specifically apropos of the romances of chivalry, which remain to this day among the great literary manifestations of esoterism in the Middle Ages:

In the *Titurel*, the legend of the *Grail* reached its final and splendid transfiguration under the influence of ideas that Wolfram[12] appears to have taken from France, and particularly from the Templars in the south of France. It was no longer in the British Isles but in Gaul, on the border of Spain, that the *Grail* was kept. A hero named Titurel founded a temple in order to deposit the holy *Vessel* there, and it was the prophet Merlin, initiated by Joseph of Arimathea in person to the plan of the Temple par excellence, the Temple of Solomon, who directed this mysterious construction.[13] The *Knighthood of the Grail* here becomes the *Massenie*, that is to say an ascetic Freemasonry,

---

10. Michael Maier (1568–1622), German alchemist and Rosicrucian. ED.

11. *Histoire de France*, vol. III, pp 398–399.

12. The Swabian Templar Wolfram von Eschenbach, author of *Parsival* [*Perceval*] and imitator of the Benedictine satirist Guyot de Provins, whom he designates under the singularly deformed name of 'Kyot de Provence'.

13. Henri Martin adds this note: 'Perceval ends up by transferring the Grail to India and rebuilding the Temple there; and it is *Prester John*, that fantastic chief of an imaginary oriental Christianity, who inherits the guardianship of the holy *Vessel*.'

whose members called themselves the *Templists*; and we can grasp here the intention of linking up to a common center, represented by this ideal Temple, the *Order of the Templars* and the numerous *fraternities of builders* which at that time were renewing the architecture of the Middle Ages. We catch here a glimpse of many openings on to what could be called the subterranean history of those times, which are far more complex than is generally believed. . . . What is rather curious, and can hardly be doubted, is that modern Freemasonry goes back step by step to the *Massenie of the Holy Grail*.[14]

It would perhaps be imprudent to adopt too exclusively the opinion just expressed, because the ties of modern Masonry with earlier organizations are themselves also extremely complex; nonetheless it is useful to take them into account, for here one can see at least an indication of one of the actual origins of Masonry. All this can help us grasp, at least to a certain extent, the means by which esoteric doctrines were transmitted throughout the Middle Ages, as well as the obscure filiation of initiatic organizations during this same period, when they were truly secret in the most complete sense of the word.

14. We touch here on a very important point, but one which we cannot treat without wandering too far from our subject: there is a very close relationship between the symbolism of the *Grail* and that of the 'common center' to which Henri Martin alludes, although he appears not to suspect the profound reality involved, any more than he understands what is symbolized, in the same order of ideas, by the name of *Prester John* and his mysterious kingdom.

14

Extra-Terrestrial
Journeys in Different
Traditions

One question that seems to have greatly preoccupied most of Dante's commentators is that of what sources to acknowledge for his conception of the descent into Hell; and this is also one of the points that most clearly highlights the incompetence of those who have only studied these questions in a completely 'profane' manner. In fact, this matter can only be understood through a certain acquaintance with the stages of initiation, and it is this that we shall now try to explain.

If Dante takes Virgil for his guide in the first two parts of his journey, the principal reason, as everyone recognizes, is doubtless his recollection of the sixth canto of the *Aeneid*, but we must add that this is because Virgil's work is no mere poetic fiction, but, on the contrary, gives incontestable proof of initiatic knowledge. It is not without reason that the practice of the *sortes virgilianae* [casting of lots] was so widespread in the Middle Ages; and if people have wanted to make a magician of Virgil, this is only a popular and exoteric distortion of a profound truth which those who likened his work to Holy Writ—even if they did so only for a divinatory usage of very relative interest—probably sensed better than they could express.

On the other hand, it is not difficult to see in this connection that Virgil himself had some predecessors among the Greeks, and apropos of this to recall the voyage of Ulysses to the country of the Cimmerians and the descent of Orpheus into the Underworld; but does the concordance we have noticed in all of this prove nothing more than a series of borrowings or successive imitations? The truth is that what is involved here has a close connection to the mysteries of antiquity, and that the various poetic and legendary accounts are only translations of one and the same reality: the golden bough [*rameau d'or*] that Aeneas, guided by the Sibyl, first goes to gather in the forest (that very *selva selvaggia* where Dante also sets the beginning of his poem), is the same bough that was carried by the Eleusinian initiates, reminding one further of the acacia of modern Masonry, 'token of resurrection and immortality'. What is more, Christianity presents us with a similar symbolism: in the Catholic liturgy it is Palm Sunday [*la fête des Rameaux*][1] that opens Holy Week, which encompasses the death of Christ, his descent into Hell, and his resurrection, to be followed shortly thereafter by his glorious ascension; and it is precisely on Holy Monday that Dante's recital commences, as if to indicate that it is in undertaking the quest of the mysterious bough that he loses his way in the dark forest where he will meet Virgil; and his journey across the worlds will last until Easter Sunday, that is to say until the Day of Resurrection.

On the one hand, death and descent into the hells; on the other, resurrection and ascension to the heavens. These are two inverse and complementary phases, of which the first is the necessary preparation for the second, and can easily be recognized in the description of the Hermetic 'Great Work'; the same is clearly affirmed in all traditional doctrines. In Islam, for example, we encounter the episode of Muhammad's 'nocturnal journey', consisting of the same descent into the infernal regions (*isrā*), followed by ascension to the various paradises or celestial spheres (*mir'āj*). There is a striking similarity between certain accounts of this 'nocturnal journey' and Dante's poem, so much so that some have seen in them one of the principal sources of Dante's inspiration. Don Miguel Asìn Palacios

---

1. The Latin name for this festival is *Dominica in Palmis* [Palm Sunday]. The palm and the bough are obviously one and the same thing; and the palm, taken as an emblem for the martyrs, also has the meaning we are indicating here. Recall also the popular name *Pâques fleuries* [for Palm Sunday, literally 'flowery Pascha'], which very clearly expresses, although those who use it today are ignorant of it, the relationship of the symbolism of this festival to the resurrection.

has shown the multiple relationships that exist in respect not only of content but also of form, between the *Divine Comedy* (not to speak of some passages from the *Vita Nuova* and the *Convivio*) on the one hand, and both the *Kitāb al-Isrā* (The Book of the Nocturnal Journey) and the *Futūḥāt al-Makkiyah* (The Meccan Revelations) of Muḥyi'd-Dīn ibn al-'Arabi on the other, works that were written about eighty years before Dante's. He concludes that these analogies, taken alone, are more numerous than all of those that other commentators have succeeded in establishing between Dante's work and the literatures of all other countries.[2] Here are some examples:

In an adaptation of the Islamic legend, a wolf and a lion bar the pilgrim's route; similarly, the panther, the lion, and the she-wolf force Dante to draw back. . . . Heaven sends Virgil to Dante and Gabriel to Muhammad, each satisfying the pilgrim's curiosity during the journey. Hell is heralded in the two legends by identical signs: violent and confused tumult, blasts of fire. . . . The architecture of Dante's Inferno is modeled on the Muslim Hell: both consist of an immense funnel formed by a series of levels, with circular steps or stairs descending gradually to the bottom of the earth; each of them harbors a category of sinners whose culpability and punishment grow worse the deeper the circle in which they dwell. Each level is subdivided into several others, allotted to various categories of sinners; finally, both of these Hells are located under the city of Jerusalem. . . . On leaving Hell, in order to purify himself and ascend to Paradise, Dante undergoes a triple ablution. In the Islamic tradition, a similar triple ablution purifies souls: before entering Heaven, they are plunged successively into the waters of the three rivers that fertilize the Garden of Abraham. . . . The architecture of the celestial spheres across which the Ascension occurs is identical in the two

2. Miguel Asìn Palacios, *La Escatologia Musulmana en la Divina Comedia: sequida de la historia y critica de una polemica* (Madrid: Editorial Maestre, 1961). [See *Islam and the Divine Comedy*, tr. Harold Sutherland (London: Frank Cass & Co., 1968).] Cf. Edgar Blochet, *Les Sources orientales de 'la divine Comédie'* (Paris: J. Maisonneuve, 1901).

legends: the souls of the blessed are ranged in the nine heavens according to their respective merits, and are gathered finally in the Empyrean or last sphere. . . . Just as Beatrice stands aside that Saint Bernard may guide Dante during the final stages, so does Gabriel abandon Muhammad near the throne of God, to which he will be drawn by a luminous garland. . . . The final apotheosis of both ascensions is the same: the two travelers, raised to the presence of God, describe Him as a center of intense light surrounded by nine concentric circles formed by close files of innumerable angelic spirits who emit luminous rays; one of the circular ranks nearest to the center is that of the Cherubim; each circle encloses the circle immediately below it, and all nine turn unceasingly around the divine center. . . . The infernal stages, the astronomical heavens, the circles of the mystic rose, the angelic choirs that surround the center of divine light, the three circles symbolizing the trinity of persons: all are borrowed word for word by the Florentine poet from Muḥyi 'd-Dīn ibn al-'Arabī.[3]

Such coincidences, extending to the most precise details, cannot be accidental, and we have many reasons to think that to a considerable extent Dante indeed was inspired by the writings of Muḥyi 'd-Dīn. But how could he have known these writings? One possible intermediary is Brunetto Latini, who had lived in Spain, but this hypothesis hardly seems satisfactory because, though he was born in Murcia (hence his nickname *Al-Andalusi*), Muḥyi 'd-Dīn did not spend all his life in Spain, dying in fact in Damascus; and though his disciples were spread throughout the Islamic world—primarily in Syria and Egypt—it is unlikely that his works entered the public domain at that time; indeed, some have never yet been published. Muḥyi 'd-Dīn was in fact anything but the 'mystical poet' that Palacios imagines him to be. What must be acknowledged here is that in Islamic esoterism Muḥyi 'd-Dīn is referred to as *al-Shaykh al-Akbar*, that is, the greatest of spiritual Masters, the Master par excellence; that his doctrine is purely metaphysical; and that several of

---

3. A. Cabaton, 'La Divine Comédie et l'Islam', in *Revue de l'Histoire des Religions*, 1920; this article contains a résumé of the work of Miguel Asìn Palacios.

the principal initiatic Orders in Islam, among them the highest and least accessible, proceed from him directly. We have already indicated that in the thirteenth century, that is to say in Muḥyi 'd-Dīn's own era, such organizations were in contact with the Orders of Chivalry, which for us explains the transmission noted. Were it otherwise, and had Dante known of Muḥyi 'd-Dīn through 'profane' channels, why did he never name him, as he did two exoteric philosophers of Islam, Avicenna and Averroës?[4] Furthermore, it is recognized that there were some Islamic influences at the beginnings of Rosicrucianism; it is to this that the supposed journeys of Christian Rosenkreuz to the East allude. But the real origin of Rosicrucianism, as we have already stated, lies precisely in the Orders of Chivalry; and it was these that formed the true intellectual link between the East and the West in the Middle Ages.

Modern Western critics, who regard Muhammad's 'nocturnal journey' as nothing more than a poetic legend, claim that this legend is not specifically Islamic, or Arab, but of Persian origin, for an account of a similar journey exists in a Mazdean book, the *Ardā Vîrāf Nāmeh*.[5] Some think it necessary to go back much further, to India, where in Brahmanism as well as in Buddhism we indeed meet a multitude of symbolic descriptions of the diverse states of existence under the form of a hierarchically organized ensemble of heavens and hells; and some even go so far as to suppose that Dante may have been directly influenced by doctrines from India.[6] For those who see all this as mere 'literature', such a way of looking at things is understandable, although it is rather difficult, even from the historical point of view, to admit that Dante could have known anything

4. *Inferno*, IV, 143–144.
5. Blochet, 'Études sur l'Histoire religieuse de l'Islam', in *Revue de l'Histoire des Religions*, 1899. A French translation of *Livre d'Ardā Vîrāf*, by M.A. Barthélemy, was published in 1887.
6. Angelo de Gubernatis, 'Dante e l'India', in *Giornale della Società asiatica italiana*, vol. III, 1889, pp3–19; 'Le Type indien de Lucifer chez Dante', in *Actes du Xᵉ Congrès des Orientalistes*. Cabaton, in the article cited above, points out that 'Ozanam had already glimpsed a double Islamic and Indian influence on Dante' ('Essai sur la philosophie de Dante', pp198 ff); but we must say that the work of Ozanam, in spite of the reputation it enjoys, seems to us extremely superficial.

of India other than through the intermediary of the Arabs. For us, however, these similarities demonstrate nothing else than the unity of doctrine in all traditions. There is nothing astonishing in finding everywhere expressions of the same truths, but precisely in order not to be astonished one must first of all know that these are truths, and not more or less arbitrary fictions. Where there are only resemblances of a general order there is no reason to conclude that there must have been direct communication, for such a conclusion would be justified only if the same ideas were expressed in an identical form, such as is the case with Muḥyi 'd-Dīn and Dante. It is certain that what we find in Dante is in perfect accord with the Hindu theories of the worlds and cosmic cycles, though it is not clothed in a properly Hindu form; and this accord necessarily exists among all who are conscious of the same truths, however they may have acquired knowledge of them.

15

The
Three Worlds

The differentiation of the three worlds, which constitutes the general plan of the *Divine Comedy*, is common to all traditional doctrines; but it takes diverse forms, and even in India there are two versions that, neither coinciding nor standing in contradiction, correspond simply to different points of view. According to one version the three worlds are the Hells, the Earth, and the Heavens; according to the other, where the Underworld is no longer envisaged, they are the Earth, the Atmosphere (or intermediary region), and Heaven. In the first, one must admit that the intermediary region is considered a simple prolongation of the terrestrial world, in much the same way that Dante views Purgatory, which can be identified with this same region. On the other hand, and taking this assimilation into account, the second division is strictly equivalent to the distinctions made in Catholic doctrine between the Church Militant, the Church Suffering, and the Church Triumphant. Here again there can be no question of Hell. Finally, a variable number of subdivisions is frequently envisaged for the Heavens and Hells, but in all such cases it is a question of a hierarchical apportionment of the levels of existence, which are really of an indefinite multiplicity and can be classified differently according to the analogical correspondences that one selects as a basis for symbolic representation.

The heavens are the superior states of the being; the hells, as the name itself indicates, are the inferior states. When we say 'superior' and 'inferior' this must be understood in relation to the human or terrestrial state, which is naturally taken as a term of comparison because it serves necessarily as our point of departure. It is easy to understand that true initiation, by which we mean the conscious acquisition of superior states, can be described symbolically as an ascension or 'celestial journey'; but one could ask why this ascension must be preceded by a descent into Hell. There are several reasons for this, but these we could not fully explain now without entering into long digressions that would lead us too far from the special subject of our present study. We will say only that this descent is on the one hand a sort of recapitulation of the states that logically pre-cede the human state and that have determined its particular conditions, and that must also partake in the 'transformation' that is to be accomplished; on the other hand, the descent allows the manifesta-tion according to certain modalities of the possibilities of an inferior order that the being still carries in an undeveloped state, and that must be exhausted before it is possible to attain the realization of the superior states. It must be emphasized moreover that there can be no question of the being actually returning to those states through which it has already passed; it can only explore these states indirectly, by becoming aware of the traces they have left in the most obscure regions of the human state itself; and this is why Hell is represented symbolically as situated in the interior of the Earth.

The heavens, on the contrary, are the superior states, and not merely their reflection in the human state, of which the uppermost prolongations constitute only the intermediary region, or Purgatory, the mountain on whose summit Dante places the Terrestrial Paradise. The real aim of initiation is not merely the restoration of the 'Edenic state', which is only a stage on a path that must lead much higher since it is beyond this stage that the 'celestial journey' really begins, but rather the *active* conquest of the 'supra-human' states; for as Dante remarks, following the Gospel, 'Regnum coelorum *violenzia pate*,'[1] and this is one of the essential differences

---

1. *Paradiso*, xx, 94 [The Kingdom of Heaven *suffers itself to move*].

that exists between initiates and mystics. In other words, the human state must first be brought to its full development by the integral realization of its own possibilities (and this is what must be understood here by the 'Edenic state'); however, far from being the end, this will be only the foundation on which the being will have to stand in order to *salire alle stelle*,[2] that is to say to raise itself to the superior states, symbolized by the planetary and stellar spheres in the language of astrology, and by the angelic hierarchies in that of theology. There are therefore two stages to distinguish in the ascension, but the first is in truth only an ascension in relation to ordinary humanity. The height of a mountain, whatever it may be, is nothing in comparison to the distance that separates the Earth from the heavens; in reality therefore it is more an extension since it is the complete unfolding of the human state. The unfolding of the possibilities of the total being is thus effected first in the sense of 'amplitude', and then in that of 'exaltation', to use terms borrowed from Islamic esoterism; and we will add that this distinction of two stages corresponds to the ancient division of the 'lesser mysteries' and the 'greater mysteries'.

The three phases to which the three parts of the *Divine Comedy* respectively relate can be further explained by the Hindu doctrine of the three *gunas*, which are the qualities, or rather the fundamental tendencies, from which all manifested being proceeds. Beings are

---

2. *Purgatorio*, xxxiii, 145. [Leap to the stars.] It is remarkable that the three parts of the poem all end with the same word *stelle*, as if to affirm the very particular importance that astrological symbolism had for Dante. The *Inferno's* last words, *reveder le stelle* [look once more upon the stars], characterize the return to the properly human state, from which it is possible to perceive a sort of reflection of the superior states; the last words of the *Purgatorio* are precisely those we are explaining here. As for the *Paradiso's* final verse, *L'Amor che move il sole e l'altre stelle* [The Love which moves the sun and the other stars], it indicates, as the final goal of the 'celestial journey', the divine center that lies beyond all the spheres, and that is, according to Aristotle's expression, the 'unmoved mover' of all things; the name 'Love' [*Amor*], which is attributed to it, could give rise to some interesting considerations in relation to the symbolism proper to initiation in the Orders of Chivalry.

distributed hierarchically in the totality of the three worlds, that is, in all the degrees of universal existence, according to which tendency predominates in them. The three *gunas* are: *sattva*, or conformity to the pure essence of Being, which is identical to the light of Knowledge and is symbolized by the luminosity of the celestial spheres that represent the superior states; *rajas*, or impulsion, which provokes the expansion of the being in a given state (such as the human), or, if one wishes, the unfolding of this being up to a certain level of existence; and finally *tamas*, or obscurity, which is identified with ignorance, the dark root of the being considered in its inferior states. Thus *sattva*, which is an upward tendency, refers to the superior and luminous states, or to the heavens, and *tamas*, which is a downward tendency, to the inferior and dark states, or to the Hells. *Rajas*, which could be represented as an extension in the horizontal sense, refers to the intermediary world, which is here the 'world of man' since it is our level of existence that we are taking as term of comparison, and which we must regard as consisting of the Earth together with Purgatory, that is, of the whole of the corporeal and the psychic world. We see that this corresponds exactly to the first of the two ways of envisaging the division of the three worlds that we mentioned previously; and the passage from one to another of these three worlds can be described as resulting from a change in the general direction of the being, or from a change in the *guna* that determines this direction by virtue of its predominance. There is a Vedic text in which the three *gunas* are presented in precisely this way, the one changing into the other in an ascending order: 'All was *tamas*: It [the Supreme *Brahma*] decreed a change, and *tamas* took the complexion [that is to say the nature] of *rajas* [intermediate between darkness and luminosity]; and *rajas*, having been commanded once more, assumed the nature of *sattva*.' This text gives a sort of schema of the organization of the three worlds, starting from the primordial chaos of possibilities, and conforming to the order of generation and the sequence of the cycles of universal existence. Moreover, in order to realize all its possibilities, each being must pass, in the particular way suited to its nature, through states that correspond, respectively, to these different cycles; and this is why initiation, which aims at the total realization of the being, must be effected through these same phases: the initiatic process rigorously reproduces the cosmogonic process, according to the constitutive analogy of the macrocosm and microcosm.[3]

---

3. The theory of the three *gunas*, relating to all the possible modes of universal manifestation, is naturally susceptible of multiple applications. One of these applications, which especially concerns the world of the senses, is found in the cosmological theory of the elements; but here we have had to consider only its most general significance, since it was only a question of explaining the distribution of the whole of manifestation according to the hierarchical division of the three worlds, and of indicating the importance of this distribution from the initiatic point of view. [The text is from the *Maitrayana Upanishad*, v.2. ED.]

16

The
Symbolic Numbers

Before passing on to some considerations relating to the doctrine of cosmic cycles, we must first make a few remarks concerning the role that the symbolism of numbers plays in Dante's work. On this subject we have found some very interesting information in a work by Rodolfo Benini,[1] who, however, has not drawn all the conclusions these appear to imply. It is true that this work is a study of the original plan of the *Inferno*, and thus primarily a literary undertaking, but the findings to which it can in fact lead have a much more considerable import.

According to Benini, there were for Dante three pairs of numbers having a symbolic significance par excellence: 3 and 9, 7 and 22, 515 and 666. For the first two numbers there is no difficulty whatsoever: everyone knows that the general division of the poem is ternary, and we have just explained the profound reasons for this; on the other hand, we have already recalled that 9 is the number of Beatrice, as seen in the *Vita Nuova*. Moreover, this number 9 is directly linked to 3, of which it is the square, and could be called a triple ternary. It is also the number of the angelic hierarchies, and therefore that of the heavens as well as of the infernal circles, for there is a certain relation of inverse symmetry between the heavens and the hells. As for the number 7, which we find especially in the divisions of Purgatory, all traditions are agreed in regarding it as a sacred number, and we do not believe it useful to enumerate here the many applications to

1. 'Per la restituzione della Cantica dell'Inferno alla sua forma primitiva', in *Nuovo Patto*, September/November 1921, pp506–532.

which it gives rise. We will only recall, as one of the principal ones, the idea of the seven planets, which serves as the basis for a multitude of analogical correspondences (an example of which we have seen in reference to the seven liberal arts). The number 22 is linked to 7 through the ratio $^{22}/_{7}$, which is the approximation of the ratio of the circumference to the diameter of a circle, so that the combination of these two numbers represents the circle, which is the most perfect form for Dante as for the Pythagoreans (and all the divisions of each of the three worlds have this circular form). Moreover, 22 combines the symbols of two of the 'elementary movements' of Aristotelian physics: *locomotion*, represented by two, and *alteration*, represented by 20, as Dante himself explains in the *Convivio*.[2] Such, in any case, are the interpretations given by Benini for this last number. For our part, although acknowledging them to be perfectly correct, we must say that this number does not seem to us so fundamental as he thinks, being derived in all likelihood from another number which the same author regards as of only secondary importance, whereas in reality its significance is much greater: the number 11, of which 22 is only a multiple.

We must in fact insist on this point somewhat, and say at the outset that this omission on Benini's part surprised us all the more as his entire work rests upon the fact that in the *Inferno* most of the complete scenes or episodes into which the various cantos are divided comprise exactly eleven, or twenty-two, stanzas (some have only ten). There are also a number of preludes and finales of seven stanzas; and if these proportions have not always been preserved intact, it is because the original plan of the *Inferno* has been subsequently modified. Under these circumstances, why should 11 not be at least as important as 22? These two numbers can be found associated again in the dimensions assigned to the lowest circles of the 'pit of Hell', the circumferences of which are 11 and 22 miles respectively. But 22 is not the only multiple of 11 that occurs in the poem. There is also 33, the number of cantos into which each of the three parts is

---

2. The third 'elementary movement', that of *growth*, is represented by 1,000; and the sum of the three symbolic numbers is 1,022, which, according to Dante, the 'sages of Egypt' regarded as the number of the fixed stars.

divided. Only the *Inferno* has 34, but the first canto is more by way of a general introduction that completes the total number 100 for the work as a whole. On the other hand, when we know how important rhythm was for Dante, we can imagine that his choice of a line of 11 syllables was not an arbitrary one, any more than was the stanza of three lines, which recalls for us the ternary: each stanza has 33 syllables, in the same way as the sets of 11 and 22 stanzas just mentioned contain 33 and 66 lines respectively; and the various multiples of 11 that we find here all have a particular symbolic value. It is quite insufficient therefore to limit oneself, as does Benini, to introducing 10 and 11 between 7 and 22 in order to construct a 'tetrachord that has a vague resemblance to the Greek tetrachord,' the explanation of which seems to us rather awkward.

The truth is that the number 11 has played a considerable role in the symbolism of certain initiatic organizations; and as for its multiples, we will simply recall this: 22 is the number of letters in the Hebrew alphabet, and we know of their importance in the Kabbalah; 33 is the number of years of Christ's terrestrial life, found again in the symbolic age of Masonic Rosicrucianism and the number of degrees of Scottish Masonry; 66, in Arabic, is the total numeric value of the name of Allah, while 99 is the number of the principal divine attributes according to Islamic tradition; and many other correspondences could no doubt be found. Apart from the diverse meanings that can be assigned to 11 and to its multiples, their use by Dante constitutes a veritable 'sign of recognition' in the strictest sense of this expression; and this is precisely where we find the real reason for the modifications the *Inferno* had to undergo after its first draft. Among the reasons for these modifications, Benini envisages some changes in the chronological and architectonic plan of the work that are doubtless possible, but for which there does not appear to be any clear proof; but he also mentions 'the *new facts* that the poet wanted to take into account in the system of prophecies,' and it is here that he seems to approach the truth, especially when he adds: 'for example, the death of Pope Clement V, which occurred in 1314, just when the first draft of the *Inferno* must have been completed.' In fact the true reason, in our eyes, is the series of events that took place from 1300 to 1314, namely the destruction of the Order of the Temple, and its various conse-quences.[3] Dante, moreover, was unable to refrain from pointing to these events when, in making Hugues Capet foretell the crimes of Philip the Fair, after having spoken of the outrage that the latter inflicted 'upon Christ through his Vicar', he continues:

Veggio il nuovo Pilato si crudele
Che ciò nol sazia, ma, senza decreto,
Porta nel *tempio* le cupide vele.[4]

What is more astonishing, the following stanza[5] contains, in specific terms, the *Nekam Adonaï*[6] of the *Kadosch Templars*:

O Signor mio, quando sarò io lieto
A veder la *vendetta*, che, nascosa,
Fa dolce l'ira tua nel tuo segreto?

---

3. It is interesting to consider the sequence of these dates: in 1307 Philip the Fair, in agreement with [Pope] Clement V, has the Grand Master and the principal dig-nitaries of the Order of the Temple imprisoned (to the number of 72 it is said, again a symbolic number); in 1308 Henri of Luxembourg is elected emperor; in 1312 the Order of the Temple is officially abolished; in 1313 the Emperor Henri VII dies mys-teriously, no doubt poisoned; in 1314 the final destruction of the Templars, whose trial had lasted seven years, takes place; and the same year King Philip the Fair and Pope Clement V die in their turn.

4. *Purgatorio*, xx, 90–93.

> I see another Pilate, so full of spite
> not even that suffices: his swollen sails
> enter the very *Temple* without right.

For Dante, the driving force of Philip the Fair is avarice and cupidity; there was perhaps a closer relationship than is supposed between two actions imputable to this king: the destruction of the Order of the Temple and the debasement of the coinage.

5. *Purgatorio*, xx, 94–96.

> *O God, my Lord*, when shall my soul rejoice
> to see Thy *retribution*, which, lying hidden,
> sweetens Thine anger in Thy secret choice?

6. In Hebrew, these words mean: 'Vengeance O Lord!' *Adonai* should be trans-lated more literally as 'my Lord', and it will be noted that this is exactly how it is rendered in Dante's text.

These are most certainly the 'new facts' that Dante had to take into account, and this for other motives than those that could occur to one who ignores the nature of the organizations to which he belonged. These organizations, which proceeded from the Order of the Temple and were to inherit a part of its legacy, had to conceal themselves with far greater care than before, especially after the death of their outward leader, Emperor Henry VII of Luxembourg, whose seat in the highest part of the heavens[7] Beatrice had shown to Dante by way of anticipation. From then on, it was advisable to conceal the 'sign of recognition' to which we have referred: the divisions of the poem where the number eleven appeared most clearly had to be, not suppressed, but rendered less visible, in such a way as to be recognizable only by those who were acquainted with their raison d'être and meaning. And if we reflect that six centuries went by before their existence was revealed publicly, it must be admitted that the intended precautions were well devised, and not lacking in effectiveness.[8]

On the other hand, at the same time that he was making these changes to the first part of his poem, Dante was taking the opportunity to insert into it some new references to other symbolic numbers; and here is what Benini says: 'Dante then thought of adjusting the intervals between the prophecies and other salient features of the poem in such a way that they would correspond to one another according to some determined numbers of lines, quite

---

7. *Paradiso*, xxx, 124–148. This passage concerns precisely the *convento delle bianche stole* [gathering of white robes]. The organizations in question had taken *Altri* as a password, which Aroux (*Dante hérétique, révolutionnaire et socialiste*, p 227) interprets as: *Arrigo Lucemburghese Teutonico, Romano Imperatore*; we think that the word *Teutonico* is incorrect and should be replaced by *Templar*. It is true however that there must have been a certain connection between the Order of the Temple and that of the *Teutonic Knights*; it is not without reason that they were founded almost simultaneously, the first in 1118 and the second in 1128. Aroux supposes that the word *altri* could be interpreted as has just been mentioned in a certain passage of Dante (*Inferno* ix, 9), and that, in the same way, the word *tal* (idem, viii 130, and ix, 8) could be translated as *Teutonico Arrigo Lucemburghese*.

8. The number 11 has been kept in the ritual of the 33rd Scottish degree, where it is associated precisely with the date of the abolition of the Order of the Temple, calculated according to the Masonic era, not the common calendar.

naturally chosen from among the symbolic numbers. In short, Dante substituted for the earlier plan a system of consonances and rhythmic periods far more complicated and *secret*, as befits a revelatory language spoken by those who see the future. Here the famous numbers 515 and 666 make their appearance, numbers that recur frequently in the trilogy: 666 lines separate Ciacco's prophecy from that of Virgil, and 515 Farinata's prophecy from that of Ciacco; 666 lines are interposed again between the prophecy of Brunetto Latini and that of Farinata, and again 515 between the prophecy of Nicolas III and that of Master Brunetto.' These numbers 515 and 666, which we see alternate so regularly, are opposed to each other in the symbolism adopted by Dante: we know in fact that 666 is the 'number of the beast' in the Apocalypse, and that innumerable, and often fanciful, calculations have been indulged in to find the name of the Antichrist, of whom it must represent the numeric value, 'for this number is a number of man.'[9] On the other hand, 515 is expressly invested with a meaning directly contrary to 666 in Beatrices's prediction: 'A cinquecento diece e cinque, messo di Dio....' [Guénon's emphasis].[10] Some have thought this 515 equivalent to the mysterious *Veltro*, enemy of the she-wolf, which is also identified with the apocalyptic beast;[11] and it has even been suggested that both symbols designated Henry of Luxembourg.[12] We do not intend to discuss the significance of the *Veltro*[13] here, but neither do we believe it necessary to see in it an allusion to a particular person; for us, it

9. Rev. 13:18.

10. *Purgatorio*, xxxiii, 43–44. ['...by God's decree, *five hundred, ten and five....*']

11. *Inferno* I, 100–111. We know that the she-wolf was the first symbol of Rome, but that it was replaced by the eagle during the imperial epoch.

12. Ernesto Giacomo Parodi [1862–1923], *Poesia e Storia nella Divina Commedia* [Vicenza: Neri Pozza Editore, 1965].

13. The *Veltro* is a greyhound, a dog, and Aroux suggests the possibility of a sort of play on words between *cane* [Italian for 'dog'] and the title of *Khan* borne by the Tartar chiefs; thus a name like *Can Grande della Scala*, Dante's protector, could well have had a double sense. This parallel is not unlikely, for it is not the only example that can be given of a symbolism resting on a phonetic similarity; and we will even add that in various languages the root *can* or *kan* means 'power', which is again linked to the same order of ideas.

concerns only one of the aspects of the general conception that Dante had of the empire.[14] Benini, in remarking that the number 515 is transcribed in Latin letters by DXV, interprets these as initials designating *Dante, Veltro di Cristo*; but this interpretation is singularly far-fetched, and moreover nothing authorizes us to suppose that Dante wanted to identify himself with this 'messenger of God'. In reality it suffices simply to change the order of the numeric letters to arrive at DVX, that is, the word *Dux*, which can be understood without further explanation;[15] and we will add that the sum of the numerals in 515 again gives the number 11.[16] This *Dux* may very well be Henry of Luxembourg, if one wishes, but it is also and by the same right any other leader chosen by the same organizations to realize the objective that they set themselves in the social order, and that Scottish Masonry still calls 'the reign of the Holy Empire'.[17]

14. The emperor as conceived by Dante is wholly comparable to the *Chakravartī* or universal monarch of the Hindus, whose essential function is to maintain peace *sarvabhaumika*, that is, extending over the whole earth; there are some parallels to be drawn between this theory of the empire and that of the Caliphate in Muḥyi 'd-Dīn.

15. We can note moreover that this *Dux* is the equivalent of the Tartar *Khan*.

16. Likewise, DIL, the first letters of the words *Diligite justitiam...*, and which are first stated separately (*Paradiso*, XVIII, 78), have the value 551, which is formed from the same figures as 515 arranged in a different order, and which also reduces to 11.

17. Certain Supreme Councils of the Scottish Rite, however, notably that of Belgium, have eliminated from their Constitutions and rituals the expression 'Holy Empire' wherever it was found. We see here the sign of a singular lack of comprehension of symbolism even in its most fundamental elements, and this shows to what degree of degeneracy certain segments of contemporary Masonry have sunk, even in the highest grades.

17

Cosmic Cycles

After these observations, which we believe appropriate for settling some important historical points, we arrive at what Benini calls the 'chronology' of Dante's poem. We have already recalled that Dante accomplished his journey across the worlds during Holy Week, that is to say at the time in the liturgical year that corresponds to the vernal equinox; and we have also seen that according to Aroux it was at this time that the *Cathars* performed their initiations. On the other hand, in the Masonic Rosicrucian Chapters, the commemoration of the Last Supper is celebrated on Holy Thursday, and work resumes symbolically on Friday at three o'clock in the afternoon, that is to say on the day and at the hour when Christ died. Finally, the commencement of this Holy Week in the year 1300 coincided with the full moon, and in order to complete the coincidences reported by Aroux, one could point out apropos of this that it is also at the full moon that the *Noachites* hold their meetings.

The year 1300 marks for Dante the middle of his life (he was then 35 years old), and for him it is also the mid-point of time; here again, we will quote Benini:

> Transported by an extraordinary egocentrism, Dante set his vision at the middle of the world's duration—the movement of the heavens had lasted 65 centuries before him, and would extend 65 more after him—and, by a clever contrivance, had the exact anniversaries of some of the greatest events in history meet in three kinds of astronomical years, and, in a fourth kind, the anniversay of the most important event of his own life.

What must hold our attention here above all is the calculation of the total duration of the world, or rather of the present cycle: two times 65 centuries, namely 130 centuries or 13,000 years, of which the 13 centuries that have elapsed since the beginning of the Christian era form exactly a tenth. Moreover, the number 65 is remarkable in itself since by the addition of its numerals it again comes to 11, and this number 11 is composed of 6 and 5, which are the symbolic numbers of the macrocosm and the microcosm respectively, both of which Dante derives from principial unity when he says: 'Così come raia dell'*un*, se si conosce, il *cinque* e il *sei*.'[1] Lastly, by transposing 65 into Roman numerals, as we have done for 515, we have LXV, or, with the same inversion as before, LVX, namely the word *Lux*, and this may have a connection with the Masonic era of the *True Light*.[2]

But what is more interesting is that the duration of 13,000 years is none other than the half-period of the precession of the equinoxes, exceeding the exact value by only 40 years (hence less than half a century), and thus representing an acceptable approximation, especially where this period is expressed in centuries. Indeed, the total period is in reality 25,920 years, so that half of it is 12,960 years. This half-period is the 'great year' of the Persians and the Greeks, and was sometimes estimated at 12,000 years, which is far less exact than Dante's figure of 13,000. This 'great year' was in fact regarded by the ancients as the time elapsing between two renewals of the world, which, in the history of terrestrial humanity, must doubtless be interpreted as the interval separating the great cataclysms during which entire continents disappeared (of which the last was the destruction of Atlantis). Actually, this is only a secondary cycle, which can be considered part of another more extended cycle; but by virtue of a certain law of correspondence, each of the secondary cycles reproduces, on a reduced scale, phases comparable to those of the great cycles of which it is a part. What can be said of the cyclical laws in general will therefore find its application at different degrees:

1. *Paradiso*, xv, 56–57. ['. . . as *five* and *six*, if understood, ray forth from *unity*.']
2. We will add further that in Hebrew the number 65 is that of the divine name *Adonai*.

143

historical cycles, geological cycles, and true cosmic cycles, with divisions and subdivisions that further multiply these possibilities of application. Besides, when one goes beyond the limits of the terrestrial world, there can no longer be any question of measuring the duration of a cycle by a number of years understood literally; the numbers then take on a purely symbolic value, and express proportions rather than real durations. It is no less true that in Hindu cosmology all cyclical numbers are based essentially on the period of the precession of the equinoxes, with which they have some clearly determined relationships.[3] The precessional movement is thus the fundamental phenomenon upon which the astronomical application of cyclical laws rests, and is consequently the natural point of departure for the many analogical transpositions to which these same laws might give rise. Limited space precludes our developing these considerations here, but it is remarkable that Dante adopted the same basis for his symbolic chronology; and we note here again his perfect agreement with the traditional doctrines of the East.[4]

We may ask ourselves, however, why Dante situates his vision exactly at the mid-point of the 'great year', and whether it is really necessary to speak of 'egocentrism' in this respect, or whether there are not reasons for it of another order. Let us first point out that if one selects any starting-point in time and then counts the duration of the cyclical period from this origin, one always ends up at a point that is in perfect correspondence with that from which one started,

3. The principal of these cyclic numbers are 72, 108, and 432; it is easy to see that these are exact divisors of the number 25,920, to which they are directly linked by the geometric division of the circle; and this division itself is yet another application of cyclic numbers.

4. Besides, there is a basic accord between all traditions, whatever their differences of form; thus it is that the theory of the four ages of humanity (which relates to a more extended cycle than that of 13,000 years) is found in Greco-Roman antiquity, among the Hindus, and among the peoples of Central America as well. We find an allusion to these four ages (of gold, silver, bronze, and iron) in the figure of 'the old man of Crete' (*Inferno*, xiv, 94–120), which, moreover, is identical to the statue in Nebuchadnezzar's dream (Dan. 11); and Dante's four rivers that flow out of Hell are not without a certain analogical relationship to those of the Terrestrial Paradise; all this can be understood only by reference to cyclical laws.

for it is this very correspondence between the elements of successive cycles that ensures their continuity. One can therefore choose the origin so as to position oneself ideally at the mid-point of such a period. This yields two equal durations, the one anterior and the other posterior, in the totality of which the full revolution of the heavens actually takes place, since all things finally find themselves in a position, not identical (to claim that would be to fall into the error of Nietzsche's 'eternal return'), but corresponding analogically to the one they had at the beginning. This can be represented geometrically in the following way: if the cycle in question is the half-period of the precession of the equinoxes, and if the entire cycle is represented by a circumference, it will suffice to trace a horizontal diameter to divide this circumference into two halves, each of which will represent a half-period the beginning and end of which correspond to the two extremities of the diameter. If we consider only the upper half-circumference, and if we trace the vertical radius, it will end at the median point corresponding to the 'mid-point of time'. The figure thus obtained is the sign $\oplus$, that is, the alchemical symbol for the mineral kingdom;[5] surmounted by a cross, it becomes the 'globe of the world', hieroglyph of the Earth and emblem of imperial power.[6] This use of the symbol in question leads one to think that for Dante it must have had a particular value; and the addition of the cross is implied in the fact that the central point where it was placed corresponded geographically to Jerusalem, which represented for him what we can call the 'spiritual pole'.[7] Furthermore, at the antipodes of Jerusalem, that is to say at the other pole, rises the Mount of Purgatory, over which shine the four stars that together form the constellation of the 'Southern Cross'.[8] This is the entrance to the Heavens, just as

5. This symbol is one of those that refer to the quaternary division of the circle, the analogical applications of which are almost innumerable.

6. Cf. Oswald Wirth [1860–1943], *Le Symbolisme hermétique dans ses rapports avec l'Alchimie et la Franc-Maçonnerie* [Paris: Dervy, 1995], pp19 and 70–71.

7. The symbolism of the pole plays an important role in all traditional doctrines; but in order to give a complete explanation, it would be necessary to devote to it a special study.

8. *Purgatorio*, I, 22–27.

the entrance to Hell is found beneath Jerusalem; and we find depicted in this opposition the antithesis of 'Christ suffering' and 'Christ triumphant'.

At first glance it may seem astonishing that we thus draw a comparison between a chronological and a geographical symbolism; and yet this is where we wanted to arrive in order to give to the preceding remarks their real significance, for the temporal succession involved is itself only a mode of symbolic expression. Any cycle can be divided into two phases, which are, chronologically, its successive halves, and it is in this form that we have envisaged them in the first place; but in reality these two phases represent, respectively, the action of two adverse and yet complementary tendencies; and this action can obviously be simultaneous as well as successive. To place oneself at the mid-point of the cycle is therefore to place oneself at the point where these two tendencies counter-balance each other. It is, as the Islamic initiates say, 'the divine place where contrasts and antinomies are reconciled'; it is the center of the 'wheel of things', according to the Hindu expression, or the 'invariable middle' of the Far-Eastern tradition—the fixed point around which takes place the rotation of the spheres, the perpetual movement of the manifested world. Dante's journey is accomplished by following the 'spiritual axis' of the world; indeed, only from there can one view all things in permanent mode, because one is oneself exempt from change, and consequently has a view that is synthetic and total.

From a properly initiatic point of view, what we have just indicated corresponds yet again to a profound truth: the being must above all identify the center of its own individuality (represented by the heart in traditional symbolism) with the cosmic center of the state of existence to which this individuality belongs, and which it takes as a base from which to raise itself to the higher states. It is in this center that perfect equilibrium resides, an image of principial immutability in the manifested world; it is there that the axis connecting all the states projects itself, the 'divine ray' that in its ascent leads directly to the higher states to be attained. Each point possesses these possibilities virtually, and is so to speak a potential center, but it is necessary that it become so effectively, through a real identification, to render possible the total development of the being at the present moment. This is why, in order to raise himself to the heavens, Dante has first of all to place himself at a point that is truly the center of the terrestrial world, both according to time and space, that is to say in relation to the conditions that essentially character-ize existence in this world.

Returning now to the geometric representation used earlier, we see again that the vertical radius, which runs from the surface of the earth to its center, corresponds to the first part of Dante's journey, that is, the journey through Hell. The center of the earth is the low-est point because it is toward this that the forces of gravity exert themselves from all sides; as soon as it is passed, the ascent com-mences, accomplished in the opposite direction and ending at the antipodes of the point of departure. To represent this second phase, the radius must then be extended beyond the center, so as to com-plete the vertical diameter; we then have the figure of a circle divided by a cross, namely the sign ⊕, which is the Hermetic sym-bol for the vegetable kingdom. Now, if one looks in a general way at the symbolic elements that play a preponderant role in the first two parts of Dante's poem, one sees in fact that they relate to the mineral and vegetable kingdoms respectively. We will not stress the obvious relation that unites the first to the interior regions of the earth, and will only recall the 'mystical trees' of Purgatory and of the Terrestrial Paradise. One might expect the correspondence to continue be-tween the third phase and the animal kingdom,[9] but this is not so, because the limits of the terrestrial world have here been surpassed, so that it is no longer possible to apply the same symbolism. It is at the end of the second part, that is to say while still in the Terrestrial Paradise, that we find the greatest abundance of animal symbols; it is necessary first to traverse the three kingdoms, representing the

9. The Hermetic symbol of the animal kingdom is the sign ⊕, which is made up of the complete vertical diameter and only half of the horizontal diameter; this symbol is in a way the inverse of that of the mineral kingdom, what was horizontal in the one becoming vertical in the other, and vice versa. The symbol of the vegeta-ble kingdom, where there is a kind of symmetry or equivalence between both hori-zontal and vertical directions, clearly represents an intermediary stage between the other two.

various modalities of existence in our world, before passing on to other states, where conditions are altogether different.[10]

We must still consider the points at the opposite extremities of the axis passing through the earth, namely Jerusalem and the Terrestrial Paradise. These are the vertical projections, as it were, of the two points marking the beginning and the end of the chronological cycle, which in the preceding diagram corresponded to the extremities of the horizontal diameter. If we let these latter represent their opposition according to time, and if those of the vertical diameter represent their opposition according to space, we then have an expression of the complementary roles of these two principles, the action of which is rendered, in our world, as the two conditions time and space. The vertical projection could be regarded as a projection into the 'intemporal', if we may so put it, seeing that it is accomplished along the axis whence all things are envisaged in permanent, and no longer transitory, mode; the passage from the horizontal to the vertical diameter therefore represents in reality a transmutation of succession into simultaneity.

But, one will ask, what connection exists between these two points in question and the extremities of the chronological cycle? For one point, the Terrestrial Paradise, this connection is obvious, since it is really this which corresponds to the beginning of the cycle, but for the other it must be noted that the Terrestrial Jerusalem is taken as the prefiguration of the Celestial Jerusalem de-scribed in the Apocalypse; symbolically, moreover, it is also in Jerusalem that the place of the resurrection and judgement that end the cycle are situated. The antipodal positions of these two points take on a new significance if we observe that the Celestial Jerusalem is none other than the very reconstitution of the Terrestrial Paradise, according to an analogy applied in an inverse sense.[11] At the 'beginning of time', that is to say of the present cycle, the Terrestrial Paradise was ren-

10. We might point out that in certain rites the three grades of symbolic Masonry have passwords that also represent, respectively, the three kingdoms, mineral, vegetable, and animal. Moreover, the first of these words is sometimes interpreted in a sense closely connected with the symbolism of the 'globe of the world'.

11. The same relationship obtains between the Terrestrial Paradise and the Celestial Jerusalem as between the two Adams spoken of by Saint Paul (1 Cor. 15).

dered inaccessible following the fall of man; the New Jerusalem must 'descend from Heaven to Earth' at the end of this same cycle to mark the re-establishment of all things in their primordial order; and one can say that it will play the same role for the future cycle that the Terrestrial Paradise does for this one. Indeed, the end of a cycle is analogous to its beginning, and coincides with the commencement of the following cycle. What was only virtual at the start of the cycle is effectively realized at its end, and immediately engenders the virtualities that will develop in their turn in the course of the future cycle. But this is a matter which we cannot pursue further without departing completely from our subject.[12] We will only add, for the sake of pointing out yet another aspect of the same symbolism, that the center of the being, to which we alluded above, is referred to in the Hindu tradition as the 'City of Brahma' (in Sanskrit *Brahmapura*), and that several texts speak of it in terms almost identical to those we find in the apocalyptic description of the Celestial Jerusalem.[13] Finally, to return to what more directly concerns Dante's journey, it is fitting to note that if the crossing of the terrestrial world ends at the beginning point of the cycle, this is an explicit allusion to the

12. Concerning these remarks there are still many other questions that would be worth exploring. Why, for example, is the Terrestrial Paradise described as a garden and with a vegetable symbolism whereas the Celestial Jerusalem is described as a city and with a mineral symbolism? It is because vegetation represents the development of seeds in the sphere of vital assimilation whereas minerals represent results that are fixed definitively, 'crystallized' so to speak, at the end of the cyclical development.

13. The comparison to which these texts gives rise is even more significant when we know the relationship that connects the Lamb [*l'Agneau*] in Christian symbolism with the Vedic *Agni* (of which the vehicle, furthermore, is represented by the ram). We do not claim that there is between the words *Agnus* [Lamb] and *Ignis* [Fire] (the Latin equivalent of *Agni*) anything more than one of those phonetic similarities we alluded to above, which may very well not correspond to any linguistic relationship at all, strictly speaking, but which are not for all that accidental. What we particularly want to speak of is a certain aspect of the symbolism of fire which, in various traditional forms, is linked very closely to the idea of Love, transposed in a higher sense as Dante uses it; and in this Dante again was inspired by Saint John, to whom the Orders of Chivalry have always principally linked their doctrinal conceptions. It is fitting to note further that the Lamb is found associated both with representations of the Terrestrial Paradise and with those of the Celestial Jerusalem.

'return to origins' that holds so important a place in all traditional doctrines, and on which, by a most remarkable coincidence, Islamic esoterism and Taoism most particularly insist. It is again a question of the restoration of the 'Edenic state', of which we have already spoken, and which must be regarded as a preliminary condition for the conquest of the superior states of the being.

The point equidistant from the two extremities just mentioned, that is to say the center of the earth, is, as we have already pointed out, the lowest point, and it corresponds also to the middle of the cosmic cycle if this cycle is envisaged chronologically, or under the aspect of succession. We can in fact divide the whole cycle into two phases, the one descending, proceeding in the direction of ever more accentuated differentiation, the other ascending, returning toward the principial state. These two phases, which the Hindu doctrine compares to those of respiration, are also to be found in the Hermetic doctrine, where they are called 'coagulation' and 'solution': by virtue of the laws of analogy, the 'Great Work' reproduces in abbreviated form the whole cosmic cycle. Here we can see the respective predominance of the opposing tendencies *tamas* and *sattva*, which we have already defined: the first is manifested in all forces of contraction and condensation, the second in all forces of expansion and dilation, and in this respect we also find a correspondence with the opposite properties of heat and cold, the first dilating bodies, while the second contracts them; and this is why the last circle of Hell is frozen. Lucifer symbolizes 'the inverse attraction of nature', that is to say the tendency toward individualization, with all the limitations inherent in it. His abode is therefore *il punto al qual si traggon d'ogni parte i pesi,*[14] or, in other words, the center of the attractive and compressive forces represented by gravity in the terrestrial world; and the latter, which attracts bodies downward (that is, toward the center of the earth), is really a manifestation of *tamas*. We note in passing that this goes against the geological hypothesis of the 'central fire', for the lowest point must be precisely the one where density and solidity are at their maximum; and on the other hand, it is no less contrary to the hypothesis put forward by some astrono-

---

14. *Inferno*, xxxiv, 110–111. ['. . . the point to which all gravities are drawn.']

mers of an 'end of the world' by freezing, since that end can only be a return to indifferentiation. Besides, the last hypothesis is in contradiction to all traditional conceptions: it was not only for Heraclitus and the Stoics that the destruction of the world must coincide with its conflagration; the same affirmation is found almost everywhere, from the *Purāṇas* of India to the Apocalypse; and we must note again the agreement of these traditions with the Hermetic doctrine, for which fire (that element in which *sattva* predominates) is the agent of the 'renewal of nature' or of the 'final restoration'.

The center of the earth thus represents the extreme point of manifestation in the state of existence under consideration; it is a true stopping-point, from which a change of direction occurs, the preponderance passing from one to the other of the contrary tendencies. This is why an ascent or return toward the principle commences immediately following upon a descent to the bottom of Hell; and the passage from one to the other hemisphere is made by skirting the body of Lucifer in a way that leads us to think that this central point is not without certain correspondences to the Masonic mysteries of the 'Middle Chamber', where it is also a question of death and resurrection. Here again we find parallel symbolic expressions of the two complementary phases that, in initiation or in the Hermetic 'Great Work' (essentially one and the same thing), express these same universally applicable cyclical laws upon which, we believe, rests the entire construction of Dante's poem.

18

Errors of
Systematic
Interpretations

Some will perhaps think that this study raises more questions than it answers, and to tell the truth we can hardly protest such a criticism, if indeed it is a criticism, for it could only be such on the part of those who are ignorant of how greatly initiatic knowledge differs from all profane knowledge. That is why from the start we have been careful to give notice that we did not intend to offer a complete account, for the very nature of the subject precludes any such claim; moreover, in this domain everything is so tightly interconnected that it would certainly require several volumes to develop as they would warrant, the many questions to which we have alluded in the course of our work, not to mention all those we have not had occasion to consider, but to which this development, were we to undertake it, would inevitably lead.

In conclusion, so that no one misunderstand our intentions, we shall only say that the points of view we have expressed are by no means exclusive, and that there are doubtless many others one could take equally well, and from which no less important conclusions could be drawn, all these points of view complementing each other in perfect concordance within the unity of the total synthesis. It is of the very essence of initiatic symbolism that it cannot be reduced to more or less narrowly systematic formulas such as profane philosophy delights in; the role of symbols is to function as a support for conceptions of which the possibilities of extension are truly unlimited, and indeed, every expression is itself only a symbol.

One must therefore always reserve a place for the inexpressible, which, in the order of pure metaphysics, is really what matters most.

Under these circumstances it will be readily understood that our claims are limited to furnishing a point of departure for the reflection of those who, taking a genuine interest in these studies, are capable of understanding their real scope, and to pointing out for them paths of research from which we believe a special benefit could be derived. If this work has the effect of stimulating other studies along the same lines, this alone will be a far from negligible result, the more so since for us it is not a question of more or less vain erudition but of true comprehension; and it is no doubt only through such means that it will some day be possible to make our contemporaries aware of how narrow and insufficient are their customary ideas. The end we have in view is perhaps far distant, but we cannot prevent ourselves from thinking of it and striving after it, even as for our part we contribute however feebly to shedding light on an aspect of Dante's work that is far too little known.

19

Saint Bernard

Among the great figures of the Middle Ages, there are few whose study is more suited for counteracting certain prejudices cherished by the modern mind than Saint Bernard. In fact what could be more disconcerting for the modern mind than to see a pure contemplative, one who always wished to be and to live as such, called upon to play a dominant role in conducting the affairs of Church and of State, and succeeding where all the prudence of professional diplomats and politicians had failed? What could be more surprising and even more paradoxical, according to the ordinary way of judging such things, than a mystic who shows only disdain for what he calls 'the quibblings of Plato and the niceties of Aristotle,' but who nonetheless triumphs without difficulty over the most subtle dialecticians of his day? All of Saint Bernard's life seems destined to show, through striking example, that in order to solve problems of an intellectual and even a political order there exist means quite other than those we have long since become accustomed to considering the only ones effective, no doubt because they are the only ones within reach of a purely human wisdom, which is not even a shadow of true wisdom. The life of Saint Bernard thus seems an anticipated refutation of these errors of rationalism and pragmatism, which are supposedly opposed to each other but are actually interdependent; and at the same time, for those who examine it impartially, this life confounds and upsets all those preconceived ideas of 'scientific' historians, who consider along with Renan that 'the negation of the supernatural constitutes the very essence of critical thinking,' something we readily admit, though for the rea-son that we see in this incompatibility the exact opposite of what they do: the condemnation, not of the supernatural, but of 'critical thinking' itself. Truly, what lessons could be more profitable for our time than these?

Bernard was born in 1091 in Fontaines-lès-Dijon; his parents belonged to the upper ranks of Burgundian nobility, and if we mention this fact it is because to this origin can be linked certain features of Bernard's life and doctrine that we will discuss in the following pages. We do not wish to imply that this alone could account for the sometimes quarrelsome ardor of his zeal or the violence he repeatedly introduced into the polemics he engaged in, qualities that were moreover superficial, for kindness and mildness incontestably formed the basis of his character. What we especially allude to are his relationships with the institutions and the ideal of chivalry, to which we must in any case accord great importance if we are to understand the events and the very spirit of the Middle Ages.

At about the age of twenty, Bernard decided to retire from the world; and in a very short while he had succeeded in converting to his views all his own brothers, as well as some of his neighbors and several of his friends. In his early apostleship, his persuasive force was such that in spite of his youth he became (as his biographer states) 'the terror of mothers and wives; friends were in fear of seeing him approach their friends.' Here already was something extraordinary, and it would surely be inadequate to attribute it simply to the force of his 'genius', in the profane sense of the word. Would it not be better to recognize here the action of divine grace, which somehow or other penetrated the whole person of the apostle and shone out abundantly from him, communicating itself through him as through a channel, to use a simile he himself was to apply later to the Holy Virgin, and that can also be applied within certain limits to all the saints?

It was thus that in 1112 Bernard, accompanied by thirty young men, entered the monastery of Cîteaux, which he had chosen because of the strictness with which the Rule was observed there—a strictness contrasting with the laxity that had been introduced in all the other branches of the Benedictine Order. Three years later, his superiors did not hesitate to entrust to him, in spite of his inexperience and unsteady health, the direction of twelve monks who were going to found a new abbey, that of Clairvaux, over which he was to rule until his death, always refusing the honors and dignities that were so often offered to him in the course of his career. The renown of Clairvaux was not slow to spread, and the abbey's growth was truly prodigious: when its founder died, it is said to have housed some seven hundred monks and had given birth to more than sixty new monasteries.

The care that Bernard brought to the administration of Clairvaux, personally overseeing everything down to the most minute details of everyday life, the part that he took in the direction of the Cistercian Order as the head of one of its foremost abbeys, the skill and the success of his interventions to smooth over difficulties that frequently arose with rival Orders—all these qualities give sufficient proof that what one calls 'practical sense' may often be united with the highest spirituality. All this would have been more than enough to fully absorb the energy of an ordinary man, yet Bernard soon saw another whole field of activity open up before him, indeed almost in spite of himself, for he never feared anything as much as being obliged to leave his cloister to mix in the affairs of the outside world, from which he had intended to isolate himself forever in order to surrender himself completely to asceticism and contemplation, with nothing to distract him from what was in his eyes, according to the Gospel, 'the one thing needful.' In this hope he was greatly disappointed, but all those 'distractions' (in the etymological sense of the word) from which he could not escape and about which he would complain with some bitterness did not at all prevent his attaining the heights of mystical life. That fact is truly remarkable, and what is no less so is that in spite of his humility and all the efforts he made to live in seclusion his collaboration was requested for all sorts of important affairs, and that although he was nothing in the eyes of the world, everyone, including high civil and ecclesiastical dignitaries, always spontaneously bowed to his compelling spiritual authority—whether this was due to his own saintliness, or to the age in which he lived, being hard to tell. What a contrast between our own age and one in which a simple monk, through no more than the radiance of his eminent virtues, could become in a sense the center of Europe and Christianity: the uncontested arbiter of all conflicts where public interest was in play, both in politics and in religion; the judge of the most renowned masters of philosophy and theology; the restorer of the unity of the Church; the mediator between the papacy and the empire; one, finally, whose preaching was to rally armies of several hundred thousand men!

BERNARD had begun early to denounce the luxurious living of most of the members of the secular clergy and even monks in certain abbeys; his remonstrations had provoked resounding conversions, including that of Suger, the illustrious Abbot of Saint-Denis, who even though he did not officially hold the title of prime minister to the King of France, was already fulfilling its functions. It was his conversion of Suger that made known the name of the Abbot of Clairvaux at court, where he was regarded it seems with a respect mixed with fear, for one saw in him the indomitable adversary of all abuses and injustices; and, indeed, he soon intervened in conflicts that had broken out between Louis the Fat and various bishops, and he protested loudly any infringements of civil authority against the rights of the Church. In truth, it was still a question of purely local affairs of interest only to a given monastery or diocese, but in 1130 events of a completely different gravity occurred that put in peril the whole Church, which became divided by a schism created by the antipope Anaclet II, and it was on this occasion that Bernard became renowned throughout all Christendom.

We need not enter here into all the details of the history of that schism: the cardinals, split into two rival factions, had elected in succession Innocent II and Anaclet II; the first, forced to flee from Rome, never despaired of his rights and appealed to the universal Church. It was France that responded first; at a council convened by the King at Étampes, Bernard appeared (in the words of his biographer) 'like a true envoy of God' among the assembled bishops and lords; all followed his advice on the question submitted to their inspection and recognized the validity of the election of Innocent II. The latter was on French soil at the time, and Suger went to the Abbey of Cluny to announce to him the decision of the council; he passed through all the main dioceses and was everywhere welcomed with enthusiasm; this momentum was to solidify Innocent's support in almost all of Christendom. The Abbot of Clairvaux then made his way to the King of England and quickly overcame his hesitations; perhaps he also had a part, at least indirectly, in the recognition of Innocent II by King Lothaire and the German clergy. He then went to Aquitaine to combat the influence of Bishop Gérard d'Angoulême, a partisan of Anaclet II; but it was only in the course of a second trip to that region, in 1135, that he succeeded in destroying the schism by effecting the conversion of the Count of Poitiers. In the interval, he had had to go to Italy, summoned by Innocent II, who had returned there with the aid of Lothaire, but who had been stopped by unforeseen difficulties due to the hostility of Pisa and Genoa; it was necessary to find a compromise between the two rival cities and to make them accept him, and it was Bernard who was given charge of this difficult mission, which he acquitted with the most marvelous success. Innocent could finally return to Rome, but Anaclet remained entrenched in St Peter's, of which it proved impossible to gain control; Lothaire, crowned emperor at the Basilica of Saint John Lateran, soon retired with his army; after his departure, the antipope took the offensive and the legitimate pontiff again fled and took refuge in Pisa.

The Abbot of Clairvaux, who had returned to his cloister, was dismayed by the news; shortly afterward came the rumor that troops had been deployed by Roger, King of Sicily, to win all of Italy to the cause of Anaclet, ensuring his own supremacy there at the same time. Bernard wrote immediately to the inhabitants of Pisa and Genoa to encourage them to remain faithful to Innocent; but this faithfulness was but a weak support, and to conquer Rome, it was from Germany alone that effective aid could be expected. Unfortunately, the Empire was ever a prey to division, and Lothaire could not return to Italy before he had assured peace in his own country. Bernard left for Germany and worked for the reconciliation of the Hohenstaufens with the emperor; there again his efforts were crowned with success, and he witnessed its happy outcome confirmed at the Diet of Bamberg, after which he made his way to the council that Innocent II had convened at Pisa. On this occasion he had to address the misgivings of Louis the Fat, who opposed the departure of the bishops from his kingdom; the prohibition was lifted, and the principal members of the French clergy were able to respond to the appeal of the head of the Church. Bernard was the soul of the council; between the meetings, as historians of the day describe it, his door was besieged by those who had some serious matter to resolve, as if this humble monk were endowed with the power to decide at will all ecclesiastical questions. Delegated next to Milan to bring back that city to the side of Innocent II and Lothaire, he was acclaimed by the clergy and the faithful, who in a spontaneous show of enthusiasm, wanted to make him their archbishop, an honor from which he extricated himself only with the greatest difficulty. He wished only to return to his monastery and did in fact go back there, though not for long.

From the beginning of 1136, Bernard had once more to abandon his solitude, in compliance with the pope's wishes, to come to Italy to meet the German army, commanded by Duke Henry of Bavaria, son-in-law of the emperor. A misunderstanding had arisen between Henry and Innocent II; Henry, little concerned with the rights of the Church, chose consistently to align himself only with the interests of the State. But the Abbot of Clairvaux was strongly in favor of re-establishing harmony between the two powers and reconciling their rival claims, especially in certain questions of investiture, in which he seems regularly to have played the role of moderator. Meanwhile however Lothaire, who himself had taken command of the army, subdued all of southern Italy; but he made the mistake of rejecting the peace proposal of the King of Sicily, who quickly took his revenge, putting everything to fire and sword. Bernard did not hesitate then to go to Roger's camp, but Roger was ill-disposed toward his words of peace; Bernard predicted a defeat for him, which in fact happened; then retracing his steps, Bernard rejoined Roger at Salerno and made every effort to turn him away from the schism into which ambition had drawn him. Roger consented to hear both the partisans of Innocent and of Anaclet, but while pretending to conduct the inquiry impartially, he was only trying to gain time and refused to make a decision; at any rate this debate had the positive result of bringing about the conversion of one of the principal authors of the schism, Cardinal Peter of Pisa, whom Bernard won to the side of Innocent II. This conversion dealt a terrible blow to the cause of the antipope; Bernard knew how to profit from this and, in Rome itself, through his ardent and convincing words, he managed in a few days to win over most of the dissidents from Anaclet's side. That took place in 1137, around the time of Christmas; one month later, Anaclet suddenly died. Some of the cardinals most involved in the schism elected a new antipope who took the name Victor IV, but their resistance could not last very long, and they all submitted on the eighth day of Pentecost; a week later, the Abbot of Clairvaux again headed home to his monastery.

This short summary should suffice to give an idea of what one might call the political activity of Saint Bernard, which moreover does not stop there: from 1140 to 1144 he was to protest the abusive meddling of King Louis the Young in episcopal elections, then to intervene in the serious conflict between the same king and Count Thibaut of Champagne; but it would be tedious to go on at length about such affairs. In summary, one could say that the conduct of Saint Bernard was always determined by the same intentions: to defend the right, to combat injustice, and perhaps most of all to maintain unity in the Christian world. It is this constant preoccupation with unity that animated his struggle against the schism; it is also what made him undertake, in 1145, a trip to Languedoc to bring back to the Church the neo-Manichean heretics who were starting to spread in this region. It seems that he had ever-present in his thought the Gospel words: 'That all may be one, even as my Father and I are one.'

However, the Abbot of Clairvaux had to struggle not only in the political domain, but also in the intellectual domain, where his triumphs were no less astonishing, since they were marked by his condemnation of two eminent adversaries: Abelard and Gilbert de la Porrée. Through his writings and teachings Abelard had acquired for himself the reputation of a most skillful dialectician; he even made excessive use of dialectic, for instead of seeing in it only what it really is, that is, a simple means to arrive at understanding the truth, he regarded it almost as an end in itself, which naturally resulted in a sort of verbosity. It also seems that, both in his method and in the very essence of his ideas, he engaged in a pursuit of novelty not unlike that of modern philosophers; and at a time when individualism was practically unknown, this defect had no chance of being considered a virtue, as is the case nowadays. And so some soon began to worry about these innovations, which tended to establish a veritable confusion between the domains of reason and faith; it is not that Abelard was a rationalist properly speaking, as has sometimes been claimed, for there were no rationalists prior to Descartes; but he did not know how to distinguish between what belonged to reason and what is higher than it, between profane philosophy and sacred wisdom, between purely human know-how and transcendent knowledge, and there lay the root of all his errors. Did he not go so far as to maintain that philosophers and dialecticians enjoy a constant inspiration comparable to the supernatural inspiration of the prophets? One understands easily why Saint Bernard, when his attention was called to such theories, rallied against them forcefully and even with an outburst of anger, and also that he should have bitterly reproached their author for having taught that faith was merely a simple opinion. The controversy between these two very different men, begun in private talks, soon reverberated loudly in the schools and monasteries. Abelard, confident of his competence in handling an argument, demanded that the Archbishop of Sens call a council before which he might justify himself publicly, for he thought he could easily lead the discussion in such a way as to confound his adversary. But things turned out quite otherwise: the Abbot of Clairvaux, in fact, saw the council as only a tribunal before which the suspect theologian was appearing as a defendant; in a preparatory session he produced the writings of Abelard and pointed out their most reckless propositions, which he proved heterodox; the next day, the author having been introduced, Bernard enunciated these propositions and called upon Abelard to either retract them or justify them. Abelard, instantly foreseeing a condemnation, did not await the judgment of the council but declared immediately that he would appeal the decision to the court of Rome; the proceeding nonetheless followed its course, and when the condemnation was pronounced, Bernard wrote such vehemently eloquent letters to Innocent II and the cardinals that six weeks later the verdict was confirmed in Rome. Abelard could only submit; he took refuge at Cluny with Peter the Venerable, who arranged an interview for him with the Abbot of Clairvaux and succeeded in reconciling them.

The Council of Sens took place in 1140; in 1147, Bernard obtained in the same way, at the Council of Rheims, the condemnation of the errors of Gilbert de la Porrée, the Bishop of Poitiers, regarding the mystery of the Trinity; these errors arose from the fact that their author applied to God the real distinction between essence and existence, which is applicable only to created beings. However, Gilbert retracted without much difficulty, so that it was simply forbidden to read or transcribe his writings until they had been corrected; his authority, apart from the specific points in question, was not affected, and his teaching remained in good repute in the schools throughout the Middle Ages.

Two years before this last affair, the Abbot of Clairvaux had had the joy of seeing one of his fellow Cistercian monks, Bernard of Pisa, rise to the pontifical throne; the new pope took the name of Eugene III and Bernard always maintained the most warm-hearted relations with him. It was this new pope who near the beginning of his reign charged Bernard to preach the Second Crusade. Until then, the Holy Land had held, in appearance at least, only a minor place in Saint Bernard's preoccupations; however, it would be wrong to think that he had remained totally indifferent to events there, the proof of this being a fact which is not usually given the weight it deserves: namely, the part Bernard played in the founding of the Order of the Temple, the first of the military orders by date and importance, which was to serve as a model for all the others. It was in 1128, about ten years after its foundation, that the order received its Rule at the Council of Troyes, and it was Bernard who, as secretary of the Council, was charged with drawing up this Rule, or at least with delineating its chief features, for it seems that it was only somewhat later that he was called to complete it and he finished its final wording only in 1131. He then commented on this Rule in *De laude novae militiae* (In Praise of the New Militia), where he set forth with magnificent eloquence the mission and the ideal of Christian chivalry, which he called the 'militia of God'. These connections between the

Abbot of Clairvaux and the Order of the Temple, which modern historians consider only a rather secondary episode in his life, assuredly had quite a different importance in the eyes of men of the Middle Ages; and we have shown elsewhere that these connections undoubtedly explain why Dante chose Saint Bernard as his guide in the highest circles of Paradise.

In the year 1145, Louis VII formulated a plan to go to the aid of the Latin principalities of the East, menaced by the Emir of Aleppo; but the opposition of his advisers had constrained him to postpone the plan's execution, and the definitive decision had been left to a plenary assembly which was to take place in Vézelay during the Easter holiday of the following year. Eugene III, detained in Italy by a revolution provoked in Rome by Arnaud of Brescia, charged the Abbot of Clairvaux to take his place at that assembly; Bernard, after having read aloud the papal bull, which invited France to the Crusade, delivered a speech that was, to judge by its impact, the most important speech of his life, all those present rushing to receive the cross from his hands. Encouraged by this success, Bernard traveled the cities and provinces, everywhere preaching the Crusade with untiring zeal; where he could not travel in person, he sent letters no less eloquent than his speeches. Then he went to Germany, where his preaching had the same result as in France; the Emperor Conrad, after resisting for a time, under Bernard's influence changed his mind and joined the Crusade. Toward the middle of the year 1147, the French and German armies set off on this great expedition which despite its formidable appearance was to end in disaster. The causes of this failure were many, the main ones seeming to have been the treason of the Greeks and the lack of cooperation between the various leaders of the Crusade; but certain critics hoped, quite unjustly, to lay responsibility for the failure on the Abbot of Clairvaux, who had to write a veritable apology for his conduct, an apology which was however at the same time a justification of the defeat as an act of Providence, showing that the unhappy outcome was not attributable to the faults of Christians alone, and that therefore 'the promises of God remain intact, for they do not contradict the rights of justice'; this apology is contained in the book *De Consideratione*

[On Contemplation], addressed to Eugene III, a book which is like the will or testament of Saint Bernard and which contains especially his views on the rights of the papacy. Besides, not all were discouraged, and Suger soon conceived a plan for a new Crusade, of which the Abbot of Clairvaux was himself to be the leader; but the death of this great prime minister of Louis VII stayed the plan's execution, and Saint Bernard himself died shortly afterward in 1153, his last letters testifying that he was preoccupied to the very end with the deliverance of the Holy Land.

Although the immediate purpose of the Crusade was not attained, must one say even so that such an expedition was entirely useless and that the efforts of Saint Bernard were spent to no avail? We do not think so, despite what may be thought about it by those historians who concern themselves only with external appearances, for there were in these great movements of the Middle Ages, which were both political and religious, more profound motives, one of which—the only one we will note here—was the wish to maintain within Christianity a keen awareness of its unity. Christianity was identical with Western civilization, which was founded at that time on an essentially traditional basis, as is any normal civilization, and which was to reach its apogee in the thirteenth century; the loss of that traditional character would inevitably follow any rupture in the very unity of Christianity of which we are speaking. Such a rupture, which was later accomplished in the religious domain by the Reformation, was effected in the political realm by the rise of nationalism, preceded by the destruction of the feudal regime; and one could say, from this last point of view, that the one who dealt the first blow to the grand edifice of medieval Christianity was Philip the Fair, the very one who through a coincidence by no means fortuitous destroyed the Order of the Temple, thereby directly attacking the work of Saint Bernard.

In the course of his travels, Saint Bernard frequently supplemented his preaching with miraculous healings, which were for the multitude like visible signs of his mission; these acts were reported by eye-witnesses, but Bernard himself never willingly spoke of them. Perhaps he imposed this reserve on himself because of his extreme modesty; but undoubtedly at the same time he attributed only a secondary importance to these miracles, considering them a mere concession accorded by divine mercy to the weakness of faith among the majority of the men, according to the words of Christ: 'Blessed are those who have not seen, and yet have believed.' This attitude was in accord with the disdain that Bernard had in general for all outward and visible show of the sacred, such as the pomp of ceremonies and the ornamentation of churches; some have even reproached him, with apparent justification, for harboring only contempt for religious art. Those who formulate this criticism, however, forget a necessary distinction that Bernard himself established between what he called church architecture and monastic architecture: it was only the latter that was to have the austerity he advocated, and it was only to the religious orders and to those who followed the road of perfection that he forbade 'the cult of idols', that is to say of forms, which he proclaimed, on the contrary, were useful as a means of education for the simple and the imperfect. If he did protest against the abuses of representations devoid of meaning and having no more than an ornamental value, he did not wish, as has been falsely alleged of him, to forbid symbolism in architectural art, for he himself made frequent use of symbolism in his own sermons.

The doctrine of Saint Bernard is essentially mystical, by which we mean that he sees everywhere the divinity of things under the aspect of love, which it would moreover be wrong to interpret in the merely sentimental sense, as modern psychologists do. Like many great mystics, he was especially drawn to the Song of Solomon, on which he commented in many sermons, forming a series that continued throughout most of his career; and this commentary, which always remained incomplete, described all the degrees of divine love, up to the supreme peace that the soul attains in ecstasy. The ecstatic state as he understood it, and which he certainly experienced, is a sort of death to the things of the world; along with such sensible images, all natural feeling disappears; everything is pure and spiritual within the soul itself, as in its love. This mysticism was naturally reflected in the dogmatic treatises of Saint Bernard, the title of one of the principal ones, *De diligendo Deo* [On Loving God], indeed showing clearly the place that love held in it; but one would be wrong to think that this was to the detriment of true intellectuality. If the Abbot of Clairvaux always wished to remain a stranger to the vain subtleties of the scholastics, it was because he had no need of the laborious artifices of dialectic; he would resolve in a single blow the most arduous questions because his thinking did not proceed by a long series of discursive operations; what the philosophers strove to reach by a circuitous route and by groping their way, he arrived at immediately, through the intellectual intuition without which no real metaphysics is possible, and without which one can only grasp at a shadow of the truth.

It is essential to call attention to one last trait in the character of Saint Bernard: the eminent place held in his life and in his writings by the cult of the Holy Virgin, something that has produced a flowering of legends and that may be why Bernard has remained so very popular. He loved to give to the Holy Virgin the name of Our Lady [*Notre Dame*], a usage that has become general since his time and that seems in large part due to his influence; it is as if he were, one might say, a true 'knight of Mary', and he truly regarded her as his 'Lady' in the chivalric sense of this word. If one compares the role that love plays in his teaching with the role it also plays, in a more or less symbolic manner, in the conceptions proper to the Orders of Chivalry, one will easily understand why we took care to mention his family's noble origins. Though he became a monk, Bernard remained always a knight, as did all those of his lineage; and by that very fact one could say that he was in a way predestined to play, as he did in so many instances, the role of intermediary, of conciliator and arbiter between the religious power and the political power, because there was in his person something of the nature of both. Monk and knight at one and the same time: these two traits were those of the members of the 'militia of God', of the Order of the Temple; they were also, and first of all, those of the author of their Rule, the great saint who was called the last of the Fathers of the Church, and whom some would see, not without some reason, as the prototype of Galahad, the perfect knight without blemish, the victorious hero of the 'quest for the Holy Grail'.

Index

167

Index

www.ingramcontent.com/pod-product-compliance
Lightning Source LLC
Chambersburg PA
CBHW021402090426
42742CB00009B/959